I0090744

卞尺丹几乙し丹卞と
Translated Language Learning

The Communist Manifesto
共産党宣言

Karl Marx & Friedrich Engels

English / 日本語

Copyright © 2024 Tranzlaty

All rights reserved.

Published by Tranzlaty

ISBN: 978-1-83566-227-4

Original text by Karl Marx and Friedrich Engels

The Communist Manifesto

First published in 1848

www.tranzlaty.com

Introduction
紹介

A spectre is haunting Europe — the spectre of Communism
ヨーロッパには共産主義の亡霊が取り憑いている

All the Powers of old Europe have entered into a holy alliance to exorcise this spectre
古いヨーロッパのすべての列強は、この亡霊を祓うために神聖な同盟を結びました

Pope and Czar, Metternich and Guizot, French Radicals and German police-spies
教皇と皇帝、メッテルニヒとギゾー、フランスの急進派とドイツの警察スパイ

Where is the party in opposition that has not been decried as Communistic by its opponents in power?
野党の政党で、権力の座にある敵対者から共産主義的だと非難されていない政党がどこにあるのか。

Where is the Opposition that has not hurled back the branding reproach of Communism, against the more advanced opposition parties?
共産主義の烙印を押された非難を、より進歩した野党に対して投げ返さなかった野党はどこにいるのか。

And where is the party that has not made the accusation against its reactionary adversaries?
そして、反動的な敵対者を非難しない党はどこにいるのか。

Two things result from this fact
この事実から2つのことが起こります

I. Communism is already acknowledged by all European Powers to be itself a Power
I. 共産主義は、すでにすべてのヨーロッパ列強によって、それ自体が大国であると認められている

II. It is high time that Communists should openly, in the face of the whole world, publish their views, aims and tendencies
II. 共産主義者は、全世界を前にして、自らの見解、目的、傾向を公然と公表すべき時である

they must meet this nursery tale of the Spectre of

Communism with a Manifesto of the party itself

彼らは、共産主義の亡霊というこの童話に、党そのもののマニフェストで立ち向かわなければならない

To this end, Communists of various nationalities have assembled in London and sketched the following Manifesto

この目的のために、さまざまな国籍の共産主義者がロンドンに集まり、次の宣言をスケッチしました

this manifesto is to be published in the English, French, German, Italian, Flemish and Danish languages

このマニフェストは、英語、フランス語、ドイツ語、イタリア語、フラマン語、デンマーク語で発行されます

And now it is to be published in all the languages that Tranzlaty offers

そして今、それはTranzlatyが提供するすべての言語で出版される予定です

Bourgeois and the Proletarians
ブルジョアとプロレタリア

The history of all hitherto existing societies is the history of class struggles
これまで存在したすべての社会の歴史は、階級闘争の歴史である

Freeman and slave, patrician and plebeian, lord and serf, guild-master and journeyman
自由人と奴隷、貴族と平民、領主と農奴、ギルドマスターとジャーニーマン

in a word, oppressor and oppressed
一言で言えば、抑圧者と被抑圧者です

these social classes stood in constant opposition to one another
これらの社会階級は、互いに絶えず対立していた

they carried on an uninterrupted fight. Now hidden, now open
彼らは途切れることなく戦い続けた。非表示になり、開くようになりました

a fight that either ended in a revolutionary re-constitution of society at large
この戦いは、社会全体の革命的な再構成に終わった

or a fight that ended in the common ruin of the contending classes
あるいは、対立する階級の共通の破滅に終わった戦い

let us look back to the earlier epochs of history
歴史の初期の時代を振り返ってみましょう

we find almost everywhere a complicated arrangement of society into various orders
私たちは、ほとんど至る所で、社会が様々な秩序に複雑に配列されているのを見出す

there has always been a manifold gradation of social rank
社会的地位には、常に多様なグラデーションがあった

In ancient Rome we have patricians, knights, plebeians, slaves
古代ローマには、貴族、騎士、プレブス、奴隷がいます

in the Middle Ages: feudal lords, vassals, guild-masters, journeymen, apprentices, serfs

中世:封建領主、家臣、ギルドマスター、職人、見習い、農奴

in almost all of these classes, again, subordinate gradations

これらのクラスのほとんどすべてで、繰り返しになりますが、従属的なグラデーションです

The modern Bourgeoisie society has sprouted from the ruins of feudal society

近代ブルジョアジー社会は、封建社会の廃墟から芽生えた

but this new social order has not done away with class antagonisms

しかし、この新しい社会秩序は、階級対立をなくしたわけではない

It has but established new classes and new conditions of oppression

それは、新しい階級と新しい抑圧条件を打ち立てたにすぎない

it has established new forms of struggle in place of the old ones

それは、古い闘争に代えて、新しい闘争形態を確立した

however, the epoch we find ourselves in possesses one distinctive feature

しかし、私たちが置かれている時代には、一つの特徴があります

the epoch of the Bourgeoisie has simplified the class antagonisms

ブルジョアジーの時代は、階級対立を単純化した

Society as a whole is more and more splitting up into two great hostile camps

社会全体は、ますます2つの大きな敵対陣営に分裂しています

two great social classes directly facing each other: Bourgeoisie and Proletariat

ブルジョアジーとプロレタリアートという2つの大きな社会階級が直接対峙している

From the serfs of the Middle Ages sprang the chartered burghers of the earliest towns

中世の農奴から、最古の町の勅許された盗賊が生まれた

From these burgesses the first elements of the Bourgeoisie were developed

これらのバージェスから、ブルジョアジーの最初の要素が発展しました

The discovery of America and the rounding of the Cape

アメリカの発見とケープの丸みを帯びた

these events opened up fresh ground for the rising Bourgeoisie

これらの出来事は、台頭するブルジョアジーに新たな地平を切り開いた

The East-Indian and Chinese markets, the colonisation of America, trade with the colonies

東インドと中国の市場、アメリカの植民地化、植民地との貿易

the increase in the means of exchange and in commodities generally

交換手段と商品一般の増加

these events gave to commerce, navigation, and industry an impulse never before known

これらの出来事は、商業、航海、および産業に、これまで知られていなかった衝動を与えました

it gave rapid development to the revolutionary element in the tottering feudal society

それは、よろめく封建社会の革命的要素に急速な発展を与えた

closed guilds had monopolised the feudal system of industrial production

閉鎖的なギルドは、封建的な工業生産システムを独占していた

but this no longer sufficed for the growing wants of the new markets

しかし、これはもはや新しい市場の増大する欲求には十分ではありませんでした

The manufacturing system took the place of the feudal system of industry

生産システムは、封建的な産業システムに取って代わりました

The guild-masters were pushed on one side by the manufacturing middle class

ギルドマスターは製造業の中産階級によって一方の側で押された

division of labour between the different corporate guilds vanished

異なる企業ギルド間の分業は消滅した

the division of labour penetrated each single workshop

分業は各作業場に浸透していた

Meantime, the markets kept ever growing, and the demand ever rising

その間、市場は成長を続け、需要は高まり続けました

Even factories no longer sufficed to meet the demands

工場でさえ、もはや需要を満たすのに十分ではありませんでした

Thereupon, steam and machinery revolutionised industrial production

そこで、蒸気と機械が工業生産に革命をもたらしました

The place of manufacture was taken by the giant, Modern Industry

製造の場は、巨大なモダン・インダストリーに奪われました

the place of the industrial middle class was taken by industrial millionaires

産業中産階級の地位は産業の億万長者によって奪われた

the place of leaders of whole industrial armies were taken by the modern Bourgeoisie

全産業軍隊の指導者の地位は、近代ブルジョアジーによって奪われた

the discovery of America paved the way for modern industry to establish the world market

アメリカの発見は、近代産業が世界市場を確立するための道を開きました

This market gave an immense development to commerce, navigation, and communication by land

この市場は、商業、航海、および陸路による通信に大きな発展をもたらしました

This development has, in its time, reacted on the extension

of industry

この発展は、その時代に、産業の拡張に反応しました

it reacted in proportion to how industry extended, and how commerce, navigation and railways extended

それは、産業がどのように拡大し、商業、航海、鉄道がどのように拡大したかに比例して反応した

in the same proportion that the Bourgeoisie developed, they increased their capital

ブルジョアジーが発展したのと同じ割合で、彼らは資本を増やした

and the Bourgeoisie pushed into the background every class handed down from the Middle Ages

そしてブルジョアジーは、中世から受け継がれてきたあらゆる階級を背景に押しやった

therefore the modern Bourgeoisie is itself the product of a long course of development

それゆえ、近代ブルジョアジーは、それ自体が長い発展過程の産物である

we see it is a series of revolutions in the modes of production and of exchange

それは生産様式と交換様式における一連の革命であることがわかります

Each developmental Bourgeoisie step was accompanied by a corresponding political advance

ブルジョアジーの発展段階は、それに対応する政治的前進を伴った

An oppressed class under the sway of the feudal nobility

封建貴族の支配下にある抑圧された階級

an armed and self-governing association in the mediaeval commune

中世のコミューンにおける武装した自治団体

here, an independent urban republic (as in Italy and Germany)

ここでは、独立した都市共和国(イタリアやドイツのように)

there, a taxable "third estate" of the monarchy (as in France)

そこには、君主制の課税対象の「第三の財産」(フランスのように)

afterwards, in the period of manufacture proper

その後、適切な製造期間に

the Bourgeoisie served either the semi-feudal or the absolute monarchy

ブルジョアジーは半封建制か絶対君主制のいずれかに仕えた

or the Bourgeoisie acted as a counterpoise against the nobility

あるいは、ブルジョアジーは貴族に対するカウンターポイズとして機能した

and, in fact, the Bourgeoisie was a corner-stone of the great monarchies in general

そして実際、ブルジョアジーは大君主制全般の礎石であった

but Modern Industry and the world-market established itself since then

しかし、近代産業と世界市場はそれ以来確立されました

and the Bourgeoisie has conquered for itself exclusive political sway

そして、ブルジョアジーは、排他的な政治的支配権を自ら征服した

it achieved this political sway through the modern representative State

それは、近代的な代議制国家を通じて、この政治的影響力を達成した

The executives of the modern State are but a management committee

近代国家の執行部は、管理委員会にすぎない

and they manage the common affairs of the whole of the Bourgeoisie

そして、彼らはブルジョアジー全体の共通の問題を管理する

The Bourgeoisie, historically, has played a most revolutionary part

ブルジョアジーは、歴史的に見て、最も革命的な役割を演じてきた

wherever it got the upper hand, it put an end to all feudal, patriarchal, and idyllic relations

優位に立ったところでは、封建的、家父長的、牧歌的な関係に終止符を打った

It has pitilessly torn asunder the motley feudal ties that bound man to his "natural superiors"
それは、人間を「生まれながらの上司」に縛り付けていた雑多な封建的な絆を情け容赦なく引き裂いた

and it has left remaining no nexus between man and man, other than naked self-interest
そしてそれは、むき出しの私利私欲以外に、人間と人間の間に何のつながりも残さなかった

man's relations with one another have become nothing more than callous "cash payment"
人間同士の関係は、無神経な「現金支払い」に過ぎなくなってしまった

It has drowned the most heavenly ecstasies of religious fervour
それは、宗教的熱情の最も天国的な恍惚感を溺れさせました

it has drowned chivalrous enthusiasm and philistine sentimentalism
それは騎士道的な熱狂とペリシテのセンチメンタリズムを溺れさせました

it has drowned these things in the icy water of egotistical calculation
それは、利己的な計算の氷水にこれらのものを溺れさせました

It has resolved personal worth into exchangeable value
それは個人の価値を交換可能な価値に分解した

it has replaced the numberless and indefeasible chartered freedoms
それは、数え切れないほどの、定義しがたい勅許された自由に取って代わった

and it has set up a single, unconscionable freedom; Free Trade
そして、それは単一の、非良心的な自由を打ち立てた。自由貿易

In one word, it has done this for exploitation
一言で言えば、搾取のためにこれをやったのです

exploitation veiled by religious and political illusions
宗教的・政治的幻想に覆われた搾取

exploitation veiled by naked, shameless, direct, brutal exploitation

むき出しの、恥知らずな、直接的で、残忍な搾取によってベールに包まれた搾取

the Bourgeoisie has stripped the halo off every previously honoured and revered occupation

ブルジョアジーは、それまで栄誉と尊敬を集めていたあらゆる職業から光輪を剥ぎ取った

the physician, the lawyer, the priest, the poet, and the man of science

医者、弁護士、聖職者、詩人、そして科学者

it has converted these distinguished workers into its paid wage labourers

中国は、これらの著名な労働者を有給の賃金労働者に変えた

The Bourgeoisie has torn the sentimental veil away from the family

ブルジョアジーは家族から感傷的なベールを引き裂いた

and it has reduced the family relation to a mere money relation

そして、それは家族関係を単なる金銭的関係に還元してしまった

the brutal display of vigour in the Middle Ages which Reactionists so much admire

反動主義者が賞賛する中世の残忍な活力の誇示

even this found its fitting complement in the most slothful indolence

これでさえ、最も怠惰な怠惰にふさわしい補完物を見つけました

The Bourgeoisie has disclosed how all this came to pass

ブルジョアジーは、この全てがどのようにして起こったのかを暴露した

The Bourgeoisie have been the first to show what man's activity can bring about

ブルジョアジーは、人間の活動が何をもたらすことができるかを最初に示してきた

It has accomplished wonders far surpassing Egyptian pyramids, Roman aqueducts, and Gothic cathedrals

エジプトのピラミッド、ローマの水道橋、ゴシック様式の大聖堂をはるかに凌駕する驚異を成し遂げました

and it has conducted expeditions that put in the shade all former Exoduses of nations and crusades

そして、かつての国々の出エジプトや十字軍のすべてを日陰にする遠征を行ってきました

The Bourgeoisie cannot exist without constantly revolutionising the instruments of production

ブルジョアジーは、生産手段を絶えず革命することなしには存在し得ない

and thereby it cannot exist without its relations to production

したがって、それは生産との関係なしには存在し得ない

and therefore it cannot exist without its relations to society

したがって、社会との関係なしには存在し得ません

all earlier industrial classes had one condition in common

それ以前のすべての産業階級には、1つの共通条件がありました

they relied on the conservation of the old modes of production

彼らは古い生産様式の保存に頼っていた

but the Bourgeoisie brought with it a completely new dynamic

しかし、ブルジョアジーはまったく新しい力学をもたらした

Constant revolutionizing of production and uninterrupted disturbance of all social conditions

生産の絶え間ない革命とあらゆる社会条件の絶え間ない撹乱

this everlasting uncertainty and agitation distinguishes the Bourgeoisie epoch from all earlier ones

この永遠に続く不確実性と動揺は、ブルジョアジーの時代をそれ以前のすべての時代と区別する

previous relations with production came with ancient and venerable prejudices and opinions

以前の生産との関係には、古くからある偏見や意見が伴いました

but all of these fixed, fast-frozen relations are swept away

しかし、これらの固定された、急速に凍結された関係はすべ

て一掃されます

all new-formed relations become antiquated before they can ossify

新しく形成されたすべての関係は、骨化する前に時代遅れになります

All that is solid melts into air, and all that is holy is profaned

固いものはすべて空気に溶け、聖なるものはすべて冒涜される

man is at last compelled to face with sober senses, his real conditions of life

人間はついに、冷静な感覚、つまり人生の本当の条件と向き合うことを余儀なくされる

and he is compelled to face his relations with his kind

そして、彼は自分の種族との関係に直面することを余儀なくされています

The Bourgeoisie constantly needs to expand its markets for its products

ブルジョアジーは、常にその製品の市場を拡大する必要があります

and, because of this, the Bourgeoisie is chased over the whole surface of the globe

そして、このために、ブルジョアジーは地球の表面全体を追いかけている

The Bourgeoisie must nestle everywhere, settle everywhere, establish connections everywhere

ブルジョアジーは、どこにでも寄り添い、どこにでも定住し、どこにでもつながりを築かなければならない

The Bourgeoisie must create markets in every corner of the world to exploit

ブルジョアジーは、世界の隅々に市場をつくりだし、搾取しなければならない

the production and consumption in every country has been given a cosmopolitan character

各国の生産と消費には、コスモポリタンな性格が与えられています

the chagrin of Reactionists is palpable, but it has carried on regardless

反動主義者の悔しさは明白であるが、それはそれにもかかわらず続いている

The Bourgeoisie have drawn from under the feet of industry the national ground on which it stood

ブルジョアジーは、産業の足元から、ブルジョアジーが立っている国家的基盤を引き出してきた

all old-established national industries have been destroyed, or are daily being destroyed

古くからある国家産業はすべて破壊されたか、あるいは日々破壊されつつある

all old-established national industries are dislodged by new industries

老舗の国内産業は、すべて新しい産業に追い出される

their introduction becomes a life and death question for all civilised nations

それらの導入は、すべての文明国にとって生死に関わる問題となる

they are dislodged by industries that no longer work up indigenous raw material

彼らは、もはや土着の原材料を加工しない産業によって追い出されています

instead, these industries pull raw materials from the remotest zones

代わりに、これらの産業は最も遠隔地から原材料を引き出します

industries whose products are consumed, not only at home, but in every quarter of the globe

その製品が家庭だけでなく、世界のあらゆる場所で消費されている産業

In place of the old wants, satisfied by the productions of the country, we find new wants

古い欲求の代わりに、国の生産物によって満たされ、新しい欲求を見つけます

these new wants require for their satisfaction the products of distant lands and climes

これらの新しい欲求は、その満足のために、遠くの土地や気候の産物を必要とする

In place of the old local and national seclusion and self-sufficiency, we have trade
古い地方や国の隔離と自給自足の代わりに、私たちは貿易をしています

international exchange in every direction; universal inter-dependence of nations
あらゆる方向での国際交流。国家の普遍的な相互依存

and just as we have dependency on materials, so we are dependent on intellectual production
そして、私たちが物質に依存しているように、私たちは知的生産に依存しています

The intellectual creations of individual nations become common property
個々の国家の知的創造物は共有財産となる

National one-sidedness and narrow-mindedness become more and more impossible
国家の一面性、偏狭さはますます不可能になる

and from the numerous national and local literatures, there arises a world literature
そして、数多くの国や地方の文学から、世界文学が生まれます

by the rapid improvement of all instruments of production
すべての生産手段の急速な改善によって

by the immensely facilitated means of communication
非常に容易な通信手段によって

The Bourgeoisie draws all (even the most barbarian nations) into civilisation
ブルジョアジーは、すべての(最も野蛮な国々でさえも)文明に引き込む

The cheap prices of its commodities; the heavy artillery that batters down all Chinese walls
その商品の安い価格。中国全土の壁を打ち破る重砲

the barbarians' intensely obstinate hatred of foreigners is forced to capitulate
野蛮人の外国人に対する強烈な憎悪は降伏を余儀なくされる

It compels all nations, on pain of extinction, to adopt the Bourgeoisie mode of production

それは、すべての国が、絶滅の苦痛を味わって、ブルジョアジー的生産様式を採用することを強いる

it compels them to introduce what it calls civilisation into their midst

それは彼らに、文明と呼ぶものを彼らの中に導入することを強いる

The Bourgeoisie force the barbarians to become Bourgeoisie themselves

ブルジョアジーは、野蛮人自身をブルジョアジーにすることを強制する

in a word, the Bourgeoisie creates a world after its own image

一言でいえば、ブルジョアジーは自らのイメージに倣って世界を創造する

The Bourgeoisie has subjected the countryside to the rule of the towns

ブルジョアジーは、田舎を町の支配に服従させた

It has created enormous cities and greatly increased the urban population

それは巨大な都市を作り、都市人口を大幅に増加させました

it rescued a considerable part of the population from the idiocy of rural life

それは、田舎の生活の愚かさから人口のかなりの部分を救いました

but it has made those in the the countryside dependent on the towns

しかし、それは田舎の人々を町に依存させました

and likewise, it has made the barbarian countries dependent on the civilised ones

同様に、それは野蛮な国々を文明国に依存させました

nations of peasants on nations of Bourgeoisie, the East on the West

ブルジョアジーの国には農民の国、西には東の国

The Bourgeoisie does away with the scattered state of the population more and more

ブルジョアジーは、人口の分散した状態をますます排除する

It has agglomerated production, and has concentrated

property in a few hands

それは生産を凝集し、少数の手に財産を集中させました

The necessary consequence of this was political centralisation

この必然的な帰結は、政治的中央集権化であった

there had been independent nations and loosely connected provinces

独立国家と緩やかに結びついた州があった

they had separate interests, laws, governments and systems of taxation

彼らは別々の利益、法律、政府、税制を持っていました

but they have become lumped together into one nation, with one government

しかし、彼らは一つの国、一つの政府にまとめられてしまった

they now have one national class-interest, one frontier and one customs-tariff

彼らは今、1つの国家階級的利益、1つのフロンティア、1つの関税を持っている

and this national class-interest is unified under one code of law

そして、この民族的階級的利益は、一つの法典の下に統一される

the Bourgeoisie has achieved much during its rule of scarce one hundred years

ブルジョアジーは、わずか100年の支配の間に多くのことを成し遂げた

more massive and colossal productive forces than have all preceding generations together

先行するすべての世代を合わせたよりも、より大規模で巨大な生産力

Nature's forces are subjugated to the will of man and his machinery

自然の力は、人間とその機械の意志に隷属しています

chemistry is applied to all forms of industry and types of agriculture

化学は、あらゆる形態の産業と農業の種類に適用されます

steam-navigation, railways, electric telegraphs, and the
printing press
蒸気航行、鉄道、電信、印刷機
clearing of whole continents for cultivation, canalisation of
rivers
耕作のための全大陸の清算、河川の運河化
whole populations have been conjured out of the ground
and put to work
全住民が地面から召喚され、働かされた
what earlier century had even a presentiment of what could
be unleashed?
何が起きるのか、という予感が湧いたのは、前世紀だったの
だろうか。
who predicted that such productive forces slumbered in the
lap of social labour?
このような生産力が社会労働の膝元に眠っていると誰が予測
したのだろうか。
we see then that the means of production and of exchange
were generated in feudal society
したがって、生産手段と交換手段は封建社会で生み出された
ことがわかる
the means of production on whose foundation the
Bourgeoisie built itself up
ブルジョアジーが自らを基礎として築き上げた生産手段
At a certain stage in the development of these means of
production and of exchange
これらの生産手段と交換手段の発展の特定の段階
the conditions under which feudal society produced and
exchanged
封建社会が生産し交換した条件
the feudal organisation of agriculture and manufacturing
industry
農業と製造業の封建組織
the feudal relations of property were no longer compatible
with the material conditions
封建的な財産関係は、もはや物質的条件と両立しなかった
They had to be burst asunder, so they were burst asunder

彼らはバラバラに破裂しなければならなかったので、彼らは
バラバラに破裂しました

**Into their place stepped free competition from the
productive forces**
その場所に生産力からの自由競争は歩んだ

**and they were accompanied by a social and political
constitution adapted to it**
そして、それに適応した社会的・政治的憲法が伴っていた

**and it was accompanied by the economical and political
sway of the Bourgeoisie class**
そしてそれは、ブルジョア階級の経済的、政治的影響力を伴
っていた

A similar movement is going on before our own eyes
同じような動きが目の前で起きている

**Modern Bourgeoisie society with its relations of production,
and of exchange, and of property**
生産関係、交換関係、所有関係を持つ近代ブルジョアジー社
会

**a society that has conjured up such gigantic means of
production and of exchange**
このような巨大な生産手段と交換手段を生み出した社会

**it is like the sorcerer who called up the powers of the nether
world**
冥界の力を召喚した魔術師のようだ

**but he is no longer able to control what he has brought into
the world**
しかし、彼はもはや自分がこの世にもたらしたものをコント
ロールすることはできません

**For many a decade past history was tied together by a
common thread**
過去10年間、過去の歴史は共通の糸で結ばれていました

**the history of industry and commerce has been but the
history of revolts**
産業と商業の歴史は、反乱の歴史にすぎなかった

**the revolts of modern productive forces against modern
conditions of production**
近代的生産諸条件に対する近代的生産力の反乱

the revolts of modern productive forces against property relations
所有関係に対する近代的生産力の反乱
these property relations are the conditions for the existence of the Bourgeoisie
これらの所有関係は、ブルジョアジーの存在条件である
and the existence of the Bourgeoisie determines the rules for property relations
そして、ブルジョアジーの存在が財産関係の規則を決定する
it is enough to mention the periodical return of commercial crises
商業危機の定期的な再来について言及するだけで十分です
each commercial crisis is more threatening to Bourgeoisie society than the last
それぞれの商業的危機は、ブルジョアジー社会にとって、前回よりも脅威となっている
In these crises a great part of the existing products are destroyed
これらの危機では、既存の製品の大部分が破壊されます
but these crises also destroy the previously created productive forces
しかし、これらの危機は、以前に生み出された生産力も破壊する
in all earlier epochs these epidemics would have seemed an absurdity
それ以前のすべての時代において、これらの伝染病は不条理に思われたであろう
because these epidemics are the commercial crises of over-production
なぜなら、これらの伝染病は過剰生産の商業的危機だからです
Society suddenly finds itself put back into a state of momentary barbarism
社会は突如として、一瞬の野蛮な状態に逆戻りする
as if a universal war of devastation had cut off every means of subsistence
あたかも、世界規模の荒廃戦争が、あらゆる生存手段を断ち

切ったかのように
industry and commerce seem to have been destroyed; and why?
産業と商業は破壊されたようです。でなぜ。

Because there is too much civilisation and means of subsistence
文明と生活手段が多すぎるからです

and because there is too much industry, and too much commerce
そして、産業が多すぎて、商業が多すぎるからです

The productive forces at the disposal of society no longer develop Bourgeoisie property
社会が自由に使える生産力は、もはやブルジョアジーの所有を発展させない

on the contrary, they have become too powerful for these conditions, by which they are fettered
それどころか、彼らはこれらの条件に対してあまりにも強力になりすぎており、それによって彼らは束縛されています

as soon as they overcome these fetters, they bring disorder into the whole of Bourgeoisie society
かれらは、これらの足枷を乗り越えるやいなや、ブルジョアジー社会全体に無秩序をもたらす

and the productive forces endanger the existence of Bourgeoisie property
そして、生産力はブルジョアジーの所有物の存在を危険にさらす

The conditions of Bourgeoisie society are too narrow to comprise the wealth created by them
ブルジョアジー社会の諸条件は、ブルジョアジー社会が生み出した富を成り立たせるには狭すぎる

And how does the Bourgeoisie get over these crises?
そして、ブルジョアジーはこれらの危機をどのように乗り越えるのでしょうか?

On the one hand, it overcomes these crises by the enforced destruction of a mass of productive forces
一方では、大量の生産力の強制的な破壊によってこれらの危機を克服する

on the other hand, it overcomes these crises by the conquest of new markets

一方、新しい市場を征服することでこれらの危機を克服します

and it overcomes these crises by the more thorough exploitation of the old forces of production

そして、それは、古い生産力のより徹底的な搾取によってこれらの危機を克服する

That is to say, by paving the way for more extensive and more destructive crises

つまり、より広範で破壊的な危機への道を開くことによってです

it overcomes the crisis by diminishing the means whereby crises are prevented

それは、危機を防ぐ手段を減らすことによって危機を克服する

The weapons with which the Bourgeoisie felled feudalism to the ground are now turned against itself

ブルジョアジーが封建制を地に堕とした武器は、今やブルジョアジーに向けられている

But not only has the Bourgeoisie forged the weapons that bring death to itself

しかし、ブルジョアジーは、自らに死をもたらす武器を鍛え上げただけではない

it has also called into existence the men who are to wield those weapons

それはまた、それらの武器を振るうべき男たちを存在させました

and these men are the modern working class; they are the proletarians

そして、これらの人々は現代の労働者階級である。彼らはプロレタリアである

In proportion as the Bourgeoisie is developed, in the same proportion is the Proletariat developed

ブルジョアジーが発展するのに比例して、プロレタリアートも同じ割合で発展する

the modern working class developed a class of labourers

現代の労働者階級は、労働者の階級を発展させた

this class of labourers live only so long as they find work

この階級の労働者は、仕事を見つけるまでしか生きられない

and they find work only so long as their labour increases capital

そして、彼らは、彼らの労働が資本を増大させる間だけ、仕事を見つける

These labourers, who must sell themselves piece-meal, are a commodity

これらの労働者は、自分自身を断片的に売らなければならず、商品である

these labourers are like every other article of commerce

これらの労働者は、他のすべての商取引品と同じである

and they are consequently exposed to all the vicissitudes of competition

その結果、彼らは競争のあらゆる浮き沈みにさらされることになります

they have to weather all the fluctuations of the market

彼らは市場のすべての変動を乗り切らなければなりません

Owing to the extensive use of machinery and to division of labour

機械の広範な使用と分業のため

the work of the proletarians has lost all individual character

プロレタリアの活動は、すべての個人的性格を失った

and consequently, the work of the proletarians has lost all charm for the workman

その結果、プロレタリアの労働は、労働者にとっての魅力を失った

He becomes an appendage of the machine, rather than the man he once was

彼はかつての人間ではなく、機械の付属物になる

only the most simple, monotonous, and most easily acquired knack is required of him

彼に求められるのは、最も単純で、単調で、最も簡単に習得できるコツだけです

Hence, the cost of production of a workman is restricted

したがって、労働者の生産コストは制限されています

it is restricted almost entirely to the means of subsistence that he requires for his maintenance

それは、ほとんど完全に、彼が彼の維持のために必要とする生存手段に制限されています

and it is restricted to the means of subsistence that he requires for the propagation of his race

そして、それは、彼が自分の人種の繁殖に必要とする生存手段に限定されている

But the price of a commodity, and therefore also of labour, is equal to its cost of production

しかし、商品の価格、したがって労働の価格も、その生産費に等しい

In proportion, therefore, as the repulsiveness of the work increases, the wage decreases

したがって、それに比例して、仕事の反発力が高まると、賃金は減少します

Nay, the repulsiveness of his work increases at an even greater rate

いや、彼の作品の反発はさらに大きくなっている

as the use of machinery and division of labour increases, so does the burden of toil

機械の使用と分業が増えるにつれて、労苦の負担も大きくなります

the burden of toil is increased by prolongation of the working hours

労働時間の延長により労苦の負担が増す

more is expected of the labourer in the same time as before

以前と同じ時間に、労働者にもっと多くのことが期待されている

and of course the burden of the toil is increased by the speed of the machinery

そしてもちろん、労苦の負担は機械の速度によって増加します

Modern industry has converted the little workshop of the patriarchal master into the great factory of the industrial capitalist

近代産業は、家父長制の主人の小さな作業場を産業資本家の

大工場に変えた

Masses of labourers, crowded into the factory, are organised like soldiers

工場に押し寄せた労働者の大衆は、兵士のように組織されている

As privates of the industrial army they are placed under the command of a perfect hierarchy of officers and sergeants

産業軍の私兵として、彼らは将校と軍曹の完全な階層の指揮下に置かれます

they are not only the slaves of the Bourgeoisie class and State

彼らはブルジョア階級と国家の奴隷だけではない

but they are also daily and hourly enslaved by the machine

しかし、彼らはまた、毎日、毎時間、機械によって奴隷にされています

they are enslaved by the over-looker, and, above all, by the individual Bourgeoisie manufacturer himself

彼らは、監視する者によって、そして何よりも、個々のブルジョアジー製造業者自身によって奴隷化されている

The more openly this despotism proclaims gain to be its end and aim, the more petty, the more hateful and the more embittering it is

この専制政治が、利得をその目的と目的であると公然と宣言すればするほど、それはより卑小で、より憎悪的で、より憤慨する

the more modern industry becomes developed, the lesser are the differences between the sexes

近代的な産業が発展すればするほど、男女間の違いは小さくなります

The less the skill and exertion of strength implied in manual labour, the more is the labour of men superseded by that of women

肉体労働に内在する技能と力の発揮が少なければ少ないほど、男性の労働は女性の労働に取って代わられる

Differences of age and sex no longer have any distinctive social validity for the working class

年齢や性別の違いは、もはや労働者階級にとって明確な社会

的妥当性をもたない

All are instruments of labour, more or less expensive to use, according to their age and sex

すべては労働道具であり、年齢や性別に応じて多かれ少なかれ高価です

as soon as the labourer receives his wages in cash, than he is set upon by the other portions of the Bourgeoisie

労働者は、その賃金を現金で受け取るやいなや、ブルジョアジーの他の部分から搾取される

the landlord, the shopkeeper, the pawnbroker, etc

家主、店主、質屋など

The lower strata of the middle class; the small trades people and shopkeepers

中産階級の下層。小さな商人、人々、店主

the retired tradesmen generally, and the handicraftsmen and peasants

引退した商人一般、手工業者、農民

all these sink gradually into the Proletariat

これらすべてはプロレタリアートに次第に沈む

partly because their diminutive capital does not suffice for the scale on which Modern Industry is carried on

その理由の一つは、彼らの小さな資本が、近代産業が遂行されている規模に対して十分ではないからである

and because it is swamped in the competition with the large capitalists

そして、それは大資本家との競争に圧倒されているからです

partly because their specialized skill is rendered worthless by the new methods of production

その理由の一つは、彼らの専門技術が新しい生産方法によって無価値になってしまったからである

Thus the Proletariat is recruited from all classes of the population

こうして、プロレタリアートは人口のあらゆる階級から徴兵される

The Proletariat goes through various stages of development

プロレタリアートは様々な発展段階を経る

With its birth begins its struggle with the Bourgeoisie

その誕生とともに、ブルジョアジーとの闘争が始まる

At first the contest is carried on by individual labourers

最初は、個々の労働者によってコンテストが行われます

then the contest is carried on by the workpeople of a factory

その後、コンテストは工場の労働者によって行われます

then the contest is carried on by the operatives of one trade, in one locality

そして、コンテストは、1つの地域で、1つの取引の工作員によって行われます

and the contest is then against the individual Bourgeoisie who directly exploits them

そして、その競争は、彼らを直接搾取する個々のブルジョアジーに対するものである

They direct their attacks not against the Bourgeoisie conditions of production

かれらは、ブルジョアジーの生産条件に対してではなく、攻撃を向ける

but they direct their attack against the instruments of production themselves

しかし、彼らは生産手段そのものに攻撃を向ける

they destroy imported wares that compete with their labour

彼らは、彼らの労働力と競合する輸入品を破壊します

they smash to pieces machinery and they set factories ablaze

彼らは機械を粉々に砕き、工場を燃やします

they seek to restore by force the vanished status of the workman of the Middle Ages

かれらは、中世の労働者の消滅した地位を力ずくで回復しようとする

At this stage the labourers still form an incoherent mass scattered over the whole country

この段階では、労働者は依然として全国に散らばった支離滅裂な塊を形成している

and they are broken up by their mutual competition

そして、彼らは相互の競争によって分裂します

If anywhere they unite to form more compact bodies, this is not yet the consequence of their own active union

どこかでそれらが結合してよりコンパクトな体を形成したと

しても、これはまだ彼ら自身の活発な結合の結果ではありません

but it is a consequence of the union of the Bourgeoisie, to attain its own political ends

しかし、それはブルジョアジーの団結の結果であり、ブルジョアジー自身の政治的目的を達成するためである

the Bourgeoisie is compelled to set the whole Proletariat in motion

ブルジョアジーは、プロレタリアート全体を動かさざるを得ない

and moreover, for a time being, the Bourgeoisie is able to do so

しかも、当面は、ブルジョアジーはそうすることができる

At this stage, therefore, the proletarians do not fight their enemies

したがって、この段階では、プロレタリアは敵と闘わない

but instead they are fighting the enemies of their enemies

しかし、その代わりに、彼らは敵の敵と戦っているのです

the fight the remnants of absolute monarchy and the landowners

絶対君主制の残党と地主との戦い

they fight the non-industrial Bourgeoisie; the petty Bourgeoisie

彼らは非産業ブルジョアジーと闘う。小ブルジョアジー

Thus the whole historical movement is concentrated in the hands of the Bourgeoisie

かくして、全歴史的運動はブルジョアジーの手中に集中している

every victory so obtained is a victory for the Bourgeoisie

こうして得られたすべての勝利は、ブルジョアジーの勝利である

But with the development of industry the Proletariat not only increases in number

しかし、産業の発展とともに、プロレタリアートの数が増えるだけではない

the Proletariat becomes concentrated in greater masses and its strength grows

プロレタリアートはより大きな大衆に集中し、その力は増大する

and the Proletariat feels that strength more and more
そして、プロレタリアートはますますその強さを感じる

The various interests and conditions of life within the ranks of the Proletariat are more and more equalised
プロレタリアートの階級におけるさまざまな利害と生活条件は、ますます平等化される

they become more in proportion as machinery obliterates all distinctions of labour
それらは、機械が労働のあらゆる区別を消し去るにつれて、より比例するようになる

and machinery nearly everywhere reduces wages to the same low level
そして、ほぼどこでも機械が賃金を同じ低水準にまで引き下げている

The growing competition among the Bourgeoisie, and the resulting commercial crises, make the wages of the workers ever more fluctuating
ブルジョアジー間の競争の激化と、その結果としての商業危機は、労働者の賃金をますます変動させている

The unceasing improvement of machinery, ever more rapidly developing, makes their livelihood more and more precarious
機械の絶え間ない改良は、ますます急速に発展し、彼らの生活をますます不安定にしています

the collisions between individual workmen and individual Bourgeoisie take more and more the character of collisions between two classes
個々の労働者と個々のブルジョアジーとの衝突は、二つの階級のあいだの衝突の性格をますますとっている

Thereupon the workers begin to form combinations (Trades Unions) against the Bourgeoisie
そこで労働者はブルジョアジーに対して組合せ(労働組合)を形作り始める

they club together in order to keep up the rate of wages
彼らは賃金率を維持するために一緒にクラブをします

they found permanent associations in order to make provision beforehand for these occasional revolts
かれらは、これらの時折の反乱に備えるために恒久的な結社を見つけた

Here and there the contest breaks out into riots
あちこちで争いが暴動に発展

Now and then the workers are victorious, but only for a time
ときどき労働者は勝利するが、それは一時的なものにすぎない

The real fruit of their battles lies, not in the immediate result, but in the ever-expanding union of the workers
彼らの闘いの真の成果は、目先の結果ではなく、拡大し続ける労働者の組合にある

This union is helped on by the improved means of communication that are created by modern industry
この結合は、近代産業によって生み出された改善されたコミュニケーション手段によって助けられています

modern communication places the workers of different localities in contact with one another
現代のコミュニケーションでは、さまざまな地域の労働者が互いに接触しています

It was just this contact that was needed to centralise the numerous local struggles into one national struggle between classes
数多くの地方闘争を階級間の一つの民族的闘争に集中させるのに必要だったのは、まさにこの接触であった

all of these struggles are of the same character, and every class struggle is a political struggle
これらの闘争はすべて同じ性格のものであり、すべての階級闘争は政治闘争である

the burghers of the Middle Ages, with their miserable highways, required centuries to form their unions
中世の市民は、悲惨な高速道路で、組合を形成するのに何世紀もかかりました

the modern proletarians, thanks to railways, achieve their unions within a few years
現代のプロレタリアは、鉄道のおかげで、数年以内に組合を

結成する

This organisation of the proletarians into a class consequently formed them into a political party

プロレタリア階級のこの組織化は、結果的に彼らを政党に形成した

the political class is continually being upset again by the competition between the workers themselves

政治階級は、労働者同士の競争によって、再び絶えず動揺している

But the political class continues to rise up again, stronger, firmer, mightier

しかし、政治階級は再び立ち上がり、より強く、より堅固に、より強大に立ち上がり続けている

It compels legislative recognition of particular interests of the workers

それは、労働者の特定の利益を立法府が認めることを強制するものである

it does this by taking advantage of the divisions among the Bourgeoisie itself

それは、ブルジョアジー自身の間の分裂を利用することによって、これを行う

Thus the ten-hours' bill in England was put into law

こうして、イギリスの10時間法案が法制化されました

in many ways the collisions between the classes of the old society further is the course of development of the Proletariat

多くの点で、旧社会の階級間の衝突は、さらにプロレタリアートの発展の過程である

The Bourgeoisie finds itself involved in a constant battle

ブルジョアジーは絶え間ない戦いに巻き込まれている

At first it will find itself involved in a constant battle with the aristocracy

最初は貴族との絶え間ない戦いに巻き込まれます

later on it will find itself involved in a constant battle with those portions of the Bourgeoisie itself

のちに、ブルジョアジー自体のこれらの部分との絶え間ない戦いに巻き込まれることになる

and their interests will have become antagonistic to the progress of industry

そして、彼らの利益は産業の進歩に敵対するものになるだろう

at all times, their interests will have become antagonistic with the Bourgeoisie of foreign countries

つねに、かれらの利害は、外国のブルジョアジーと敵対するものとなるであろう

In all these battles it sees itself compelled to appeal to the Proletariat, and asks for its help

これらすべての闘争において、プロレタリアートに訴えざるを得ないと考え、プロレタリアートに助けを求める

and thus, it will feel compelled to drag it into the political arena

それゆえ、政治の場に引きずり込まざるを得ないと感じるだろう

The Bourgeoisie itself, therefore, supplies the Proletariat with its own instruments of political and general education

したがって、ブルジョアジー自身が、プロレタリアートに独自の政治的および一般教育の手段を供給している

in other words, it furnishes the Proletariat with weapons for fighting the Bourgeoisie

言い換えれば、それはプロレタリアートにブルジョアジーと戦うための武器を提供するのである

Further, as we have already seen, entire sections of the ruling classes are precipitated into the Proletariat

さらに、すでに見てきたように、支配階級の全部門がプロレタリアートに沈殿している

the advance of industry sucks them into the Proletariat

産業の進歩は彼らをプロレタリアートに吸い込む

or, at least, they are threatened in their conditions of existence

あるいは、少なくとも、彼らはその存在条件において脅かされている

These also supply the Proletariat with fresh elements of enlightenment and progress

これらはまた、プロレタリアートに啓蒙と進歩の新鮮な要素

を供給する

Finally, in times when the class struggle nears the decisive hour

最後に、階級闘争が決定的な時に近づくとき

the process of dissolution going on within the ruling class

支配階級の中で進行する解体プロセス

in fact, the dissolution going on within the ruling class will be felt within the whole range of society

実際、支配階級の中で起きている解体は、社会のあらゆる範囲で感じられるでしょう

it will take on such a violent, glaring character, that a small section of the ruling class cuts itself adrift

それは、支配階級のごく一部が自らを漂流させるほどの暴力的で、あからさまな性格を帯びるだろう

and that ruling class will join the revolutionary class

そして、その支配階級は革命階級に加わるだろう

the revolutionary class being the class that holds the future in its hands

革命的階級は、未来をその手に握る階級である

Just as at an earlier period, a section of the nobility went over to the Bourgeoisie

以前の時代と同じように、貴族の一部はブルジョアジーに寝返った

the same way a portion of the Bourgeoisie will go over to the Proletariat

ブルジョアジーの一部がプロレタリアートに寝返るのと同じように

in particular, a portion of the Bourgeoisie will go over to a portion of the Bourgeoisie ideologists

とくに、ブルジョアジーの一部は、ブルジョアジーのイデオロギー論者の一部に渡るであろう

Bourgeoisie ideologists who have raised themselves to the level of comprehending theoretically the historical movement as a whole

ブルジョアジー・イデオロギーは、歴史運動全体を理論的に理解するレベルにまで高めた

Of all the classes that stand face to face with the Bourgeoisie

today, the Proletariat alone is a really revolutionary class
こんにちにブルジョアジーと対峙するすべての階級の中で、
プロレタリアートだけがまことに革命的な階級である
The other classes decay and finally disappear in the face of Modern Industry
他の階級は衰退し、近代産業を前にしてついに消滅する
the Proletariat is its special and essential product
プロレタリアートは、その特別で不可欠な生産物である
The lower middle class, the small manufacturer, the shopkeeper, the artisan, the peasant
下層中産階級、小規模製造業者、商店主、職人、農民
all these fight against the Bourgeoisie
これらすべてがブルジョアジーと闘う
they fight as fractions of the middle class to save themselves from extinction
彼らは絶滅から自分たちを救うために中産階級の一部分として戦う
They are therefore not revolutionary, but conservative
したがって、彼らは革命的ではなく、保守的です
Nay more, they are reactionary, for they try to roll back the wheel of history
いや、それどころか、彼らは反動的だ、なぜなら、彼らは歴史の歯車を巻き戻そうとしているからだ
If by chance they are revolutionary, they are so only in view of their impending transfer into the Proletariat
もし彼らがたまたま革命的であるとすれば、それはプロレタリアートへの差し迫った転向を視野に入れたからにすぎない
they thus defend not their present, but their future interests
したがって、彼らは現在の利益ではなく、将来の利益を擁護します
they desert their own standpoint to place themselves at that of the Proletariat
彼らは自らの立場を捨てて、プロレタリアートの立場に身を置く
The "dangerous class," the social scum, that passively rotting mass thrown off by the lowest layers of old society
「危険な階級」、社会のクズ、古い社会の最下層によって放

り出された受動的に腐敗した大衆

they may, here and there, be swept into the movement by a proletarian revolution

かれらは、あちこちで、プロレタリア革命によって運動に押し流されるかもしれない

its conditions of life, however, prepare it far more for the part of a bribed tool of reactionary intrigue

しかし、その生活条件は、賄賂をもらった反動的な陰謀の道具としての役割をはるかに満たしている

In the conditions of the Proletariat, those of old society at large are already virtually swamped

プロレタリアートの諸条件では、旧社会一般の諸条件は、すでに事実上、圧倒されている

The proletarian is without property

プロレタリアは財産をもたない

his relation to his wife and children has no longer anything in common with the Bourgeoisie's family-relations

彼の妻や子供との関係は、もはやブルジョアジーの家族関係とは何の共通点もない

modern industrial labour, modern subjection to capital, the same in England as in France, in America as in Germany

近代的産業労働、近代的資本への服従、イギリスでもフランスでも、アメリカでもドイツでも同じ

his condition in society has stripped him of every trace of national character

社会における彼の状態は、彼から国民性のあらゆる側面を剥ぎ取った

Law, morality, religion, are to him so many Bourgeoisie prejudices

法律、道徳、宗教は、彼にとって非常に多くのブルジョアジーの偏見です

and behind these prejudices lurk in ambush just as many Bourgeoisie interests

そして、これらの偏見の背後には、多くのブルジョアジーの利益と同じように待ち伏せに潜んでいる

All the preceding classes that got the upper hand, sought to fortify their already acquired status

優位に立った先行するすべての階級は、すでに獲得した地位を強化しようとしました

they did this by subjecting society at large to their conditions of appropriation

彼らは、社会全体を彼らの流用条件に服従させることによってこれを行いました

The proletarians cannot become masters of the productive forces of society

プロレタリアは、社会の生産力の主人にはなれない

it can only do this by abolishing their own previous mode of appropriation

これは、以前の流用方法を廃止することによってのみ行うことができます

and thereby it also abolishes every other previous mode of appropriation

そして、それによって、それはまた、他のすべての以前の流用様式を廃止する

They have nothing of their own to secure and to fortify

彼らには、確保し、強化するものが何もない

their mission is to destroy all previous securities for, and insurances of, individual property

彼らの使命は、個々の財産の以前のすべての証券と保険を破壊することです

All previous historical movements were movements of minorities

それ以前の歴史的運動はすべてマイノリティの運動だった

or they were movements in the interests of minorities

あるいは、マイノリティの利益のための運動だった

The proletarian movement is the self-conscious, independent movement of the immense majority

プロレタリア運動は、圧倒的多数派の自覚的で独立した運動である

and it is a movement in the interests of the immense majority

そして、それは圧倒的多数の利益のための運動です

The Proletariat, the lowest stratum of our present society

プロレタリアート、現代社会の最下層

it cannot stir or raise itself up without the whole superincumbent strata of official society being sprung into the air

それは、公式社会の超現職の階層全体が空中に跳ね出されることなしには、自分自身を攪拌したり、立ち上がらせたりすることはできない

Though not in substance, yet in form, the struggle of the Proletariat with the Bourgeoisie is at first a national struggle

プロレタリアートとブルジョアジーとの闘争は、実質的にはそうではないが、形式的には、まず民族闘争である

The Proletariat of each country must, of course, first of all settle matters with its own Bourgeoisie

もちろん、各国のプロレタリアートは、まず第一に自国のブルジョアジーと問題を解決しなければならない

In depicting the most general phases of the development of the Proletariat, we traced the more or less veiled civil war

プロレタリアートの発展の最も一般的な段階を描写するにあたって、われわれは多かれ少なかれベールに包まれた内戦をたどった

this civil is raging within existing society

この市民は、既存の社会の中で猛威を振るっています

it will rage up to the point where that war breaks out into open revolution

それは、その戦争が公然たる革命に勃発するところまで激怒するだろう

and then the violent overthrow of the Bourgeoisie lays the foundation for the sway of the Proletariat

そして、ブルジョアジーの暴力的打倒が、プロレタリアートの支配の基礎を築く

Hitherto, every form of society has been based, as we have already seen, on the antagonism of oppressing and oppressed classes

これまで、社会のあらゆる形態は、すでに見てきたように、抑圧階級と被抑圧階級の対立に基づいてきた

But in order to oppress a class, certain conditions must be assured to it

しかし、階級を抑圧するためには、一定の条件が保証されな

け ればならない

the class must be kept under conditions in which it can, at least, continue its slavish existence

階級は、少なくとも奴隷的な存在を維持できる条件のもとに保たれなければならない

The serf, in the period of serfdom, raised himself to membership in the commune

農奴は、農奴制の時代には、コミューンのメンバーにまで上り詰めた

just as the petty Bourgeoisie, under the yoke of feudal absolutism, managed to develop into a Bourgeoisie

小ブルジョアジーが、封建的絶対主義のくびきの下で、なんとかブルジョアジーに発展したように

The modern labourer, on the contrary, instead of rising with the progress of industry, sinks deeper and deeper

それどころか、現代の労働者は、産業の進歩とともに上昇するどころか、ますます深く沈んでいく

he sinks below the conditions of existence of his own class

彼は、自分の階級の存在条件の下に沈む

He becomes a pauper, and pauperism develops more rapidly than population and wealth

彼は貧乏人になり、貧乏人は人口や富よりも急速に発展します

And here it becomes evident, that the Bourgeoisie is unfit any longer to be the ruling class in society

そしてここで、ブルジョアジーはもはや社会の支配階級になるのにふさわしくないということが明らかになる

and it is unfit to impose its conditions of existence upon society as an over-riding law

そして、その存在条件を最優先の法律として社会に押し付けるのは不適切です

It is unfit to rule because it is incompetent to assure an existence to its slave within his slavery

なぜなら、奴隷の奴隷状態の中でその存在を保証する能力がないからである

because it cannot help letting him sink into such a state, that it has to feed him, instead of being fed by him

なぜなら、それは彼をそのような状態に沈ませずにはいられ
ないからであり、彼によって養われるのではなく、彼を養わ
なければならないからである

Society can no longer live under this Bourgeoisie
社会はもはやこのブルジョアジーの下では生きていけない

**in other words, its existence is no longer compatible with
society**
つまり、その存在はもはや社会と両立しない

**The essential condition for the existence, and for the sway of
the Bourgeoisie class, is the formation and augmentation of
capital**
ブルジョア階級の存在と支配の本質的条件は、資本の形成と
増大である

the condition for capital is wage-labour
資本の条件は賃労働である

**Wage-labour rests exclusively on competition between the
labourers**
賃労働はもっぱら労働者間の競争に依拠している

**The advance of industry, whose involuntary promoter is the
Bourgeoisie, replaces the isolation of the labourers**
ブルジョアジーを非自発的に推進する産業の進歩は、労働者
の孤立に取って代わる

**due to competition, due to their revolutionary combination,
due to association**
競争のせいで、彼らの革命的な組み合わせのせいで、連想の
せいで

**The development of Modern Industry cuts from under its
feet the very foundation on which the Bourgeoisie produces
and appropriates products**
近代産業の発展は、ブルジョアジーが生産物を生産し、充当
する基盤そのものを、その足元から切り捨てる

**What the Bourgeoisie produces, above all, is its own grave-
diggers**
ブルジョアジーが生み出すのは、何よりもまず、ブルジョア
ジー自身の墓掘り人である

**The fall of the Bourgeoisie and the victory of the Proletariat
are equally inevitable**

ブルジョアジーの没落もプロレタリアートの勝利も、等しく
必然である

Proletarians and Communists
プロレタリアと共産主義者

In what relation do the Communists stand to the proletarians as a whole?
共産主義者はプロレタリア階級全体に対してどのような関係にあるのか。

The Communists do not form a separate party opposed to other working-class parties
共産党は、他の労働者階級の政党に対抗する独立した政党を結成していない

They have no interests separate and apart from those of the proletariat as a whole
かれらは、プロレタリアート全体の利害から分離し、分離した利害をもたない

They do not set up any sectarian principles of their own, by which to shape and mould the proletarian movement
かれらは、プロレタリア運動を形作り、形成するための、彼ら自身のいかなるセクト主義的原則も打ち立てない

The Communists are distinguished from the other working-class parties by only two things
共産党が他の労働者階級の政党と区別されるのは、たった二つの点である

Firstly, they point out and bring to the front the common interests of the entire proletariat, independently of all nationality
第一に、彼らは、すべての民族とは無関係に、プロレタリアート全体の共通の利益を指摘し、前面に出す

this they do in the national struggles of the proletarians of the different countries
かれらは、かれらが、かれらのかれらの民族闘争において、かれらをなすのである

Secondly, they always and everywhere represent the interests of the movement as a whole
第二に、彼らはいつでもどこでも運動全体の利益を代表しています

this they do in the various stages of development, which the

struggle of the working class against the Bourgeoisie has to pass through

これは、労働者階級のブルジョアジーに対する闘争が通過しなければならない発展のさまざまな段階において行われる

The Communists, therefore, are on the one hand, practically, the most advanced and resolute section of the working-class parties of every country

したがって、共産党員は、一方では、事実上、すべての国の労働者階級の政党の中で最も進歩的で断固とした部分である

they are that section of the working class which pushes forward all others

彼らは労働者階級のその部分であり、他のすべてのものを推し進めている

theoretically, they also have the advantage of clearly understanding the line of march

理論的には、行進のラインを明確に理解できるという利点もあります

this they understand better compared the great mass of the proletariat

このことは、プロレタリアートの大衆に比べれば、よりよく理解できる

they understand the conditions, and the ultimate general results of the proletarian movement

かれらは、プロレタリア運動の諸条件と究極的一般的結果を理解している

The immediate aim of the Communist is the same as that of all the other proletarian parties

共産党の当面の目標は、他のすべてのプロレタリア政党のそれと同じである

their aim is the formation of the proletariat into a class

彼らの目的は、プロレタリアートを階級に形成することである

they aim to overthrow the Bourgeoisie supremacy

彼らはブルジョアジー至上主義の打倒を目指している

the strive for the conquest of political power by the proletariat

プロレタリアートによる政治権力の征服の努力

The theoretical conclusions of the Communists are in no way based on ideas or principles of reformers

共産主義者の理論的結論は、決して改革者の思想や原則に基づいていない

it wasn't would-be universal reformers that invented or discovered the theoretical conclusions of the Communists

共産主義者の理論的結論を発明したり発見したりしたのは、普遍的な改革者ではなかった

They merely express, in general terms, actual relations springing from an existing class struggle

それらは、一般的な言葉で、既存の階級闘争から生じる実際の関係を表現しているにすぎない

and they describe the historical movement going on under our very eyes that have created this class struggle

そして彼らは、この階級闘争を生み出した、まさに私たちの目の前で起こっている歴史的な運動を描写しています

The abolition of existing property relations is not at all a distinctive feature of Communism

既存の所有関係の廃止は、共産主義の特徴ではない

All property relations in the past have continually been subject to historical change

過去のすべての財産関係は、常に歴史的変化の影響を受けてきました

and these changes were consequent upon the change in historical conditions

そして、これらの変化は、歴史的条件の変化の結果であった

The French Revolution, for example, abolished feudal property in favour of Bourgeoisie property

たとえば、フランス革命は、ブルジョアジーの財産を支持して封建的財産を廃止しました

The distinguishing feature of Communism is not the abolition of property, generally

共産主義の際立った特徴は、一般的に財産の廃止ではありません

but the distinguishing feature of Communism is the abolition of Bourgeoisie property

しかし、共産主義の際立った特徴は、ブルジョアジーの財産

の廃止である

But modern Bourgeoisie private property is the final and most complete expression of the system of producing and appropriating products

しかし、近代ブルジョアジーの私有財産は、生産物を生産し、流用するシステムの最終的かつ最も完全な表現である

it is the final state of a system that is based on class antagonisms, where class antagonism is the exploitation of the many by the few

それは、階級対立に基づくシステムの最終状態であり、階級対立は少数者による多数者の搾取である

In this sense, the theory of the Communists may be summed up in the single sentence; the Abolition of private property

この意味で、共産主義者の理論は一文に要約されるかもしれません。私有財産の廃止

We Communists have been reproached with the desire of abolishing the right of personally acquiring property

われわれ共産党員は、個人的財産取得権を廃止したいという願望をもって非難されてきた

it is claimed that this property is the fruit of a man's own labour

この財産は、人間自身の労働の成果であると主張されています

and this property is alleged to be the groundwork of all personal freedom, activity and independence.

そして、この財産は、すべての個人の自由、活動、独立の基礎であると主張されています。

"Hard-won, self-acquired, self-earned property!"

「苦労して手に入れた、自分で手に入れた、自分で稼いだ財産!」

Do you mean the property of the petty artisan and of the small peasant?

小商人や小農民の所有物のことですか?

Do you mean a form of property that preceded the Bourgeoisie form?

ブルジョアジーの形態に先行する財産の形態のことを言っているのですか?

There is no need to abolish that, the development of industry has to a great extent already destroyed it
それを廃止する必要はなく、産業の発展はすでにかなりの程度それを破壊しています

and development of industry is still destroying it daily
そして、産業の発展は今もなお日々それを破壊しています

Or do you mean modern Bourgeoisie private property?
それとも、現代のブルジョアジーの私有財産のことですか?

But does wage-labour create any property for the labourer?
しかし、賃労働は労働者のために何らかの財産を創造するだろうか。

no, wage labour creates not one bit of this kind of property!
いや、賃労働はこの種の財産を少しも生み出さない!

what wage labour does create is capital; that kind of property which exploits wage-labour
賃労働が生み出すのは資本である。賃労働を搾取する財産

capital cannot increase except upon condition of begetting a new supply of wage-labour for fresh exploitation
資本は、新たな搾取のための賃労働の新たな供給を生むという条件によらなければ、増加しない

Property, in its present form, is based on the antagonism of capital and wage-labour
現在の形態の財産は、資本と賃労働の対立に基づいている

Let us examine both sides of this antagonism
この拮抗の両面を調べてみましょう

To be a capitalist is to have not only a purely personal status
資本家であるということは、純粋に個人的な地位を持つことだけではない

instead, to be a capitalist is also to have a social status in production
そうではなく、資本家であることは、生産において社会的地位を持つことでもある

because capital is a collective product; only by the united action of many members can it be set in motion
なぜなら、資本は集合的な生産物だからです。多くのメンバーの団結した行動によってのみ、それは動き出すことができます

but this united action is a last resort, and actually requires all members of society

しかし、この団結した行動は最後の手段であり、実際にはすべての社会の構成員が必要です

Capital does get converted into the property of all members of society

資本は社会のすべての構成員の所有物に転換される

but Capital is, therefore, not a personal power; it is a social power

しかし、それゆえ、資本は人格的な力ではない。それは社会的な力です

so when capital is converted into social property, personal property is not thereby transformed into social property

したがって、資本が社会的所有に転化されるとき、個人所有はそれによって社会的所有に転化されない

It is only the social character of the property that is changed, and loses its class-character

変更されるのは財産の社会的性格だけであり、その階級的性格を失う

Let us now look at wage-labour

次に、賃労働について見てみましょう

The average price of wage-labour is the minimum wage, i.e., that quantum of the means of subsistence

賃労働の平均価格は最低賃金、すなわち生存手段の数量である

this wage is absolutely requisite in bare existence as a labourer

この賃金は、労働者としての最低限の存在において絶対的に必要である

What, therefore, the wage-labourer appropriates by means of his labour, merely suffices to prolong and reproduce a bare existence

それゆえ、賃労働者が自分の労働によって充当するものは、裸の存在を延ばし、再生産するだけで十分である

We by no means intend to abolish this personal appropriation of the products of labour

われわれは、この労働生産物の個人的収用を廃止するつもり

は決してない

an appropriation that is made for the maintenance and reproduction of human life

人間の生命の維持と再生産のためになされる充当

such personal appropriation of the products of labour leave no surplus wherewith to command the labour of others

労働生産物のそのような個人的充当は、他人の労働を命じる余剰を残さない

All that we want to do away with, is the miserable character of this appropriation

私たちが取り除きたいのは、この流用の惨めな性格だけです

the appropriation under which the labourer lives merely to increase capital

労働者が単に資本を増やすためだけに生活する歳出

he is allowed to live only in so far as the interest of the ruling class requires it

彼は、支配階級の利益がそれを必要とする限りにおいてのみ、生きることを許されている

In Bourgeoisie society, living labour is but a means to increase accumulated labour

ブルジョアジー社会では、生活労働は蓄積された労働を増やす手段にすぎない

In Communist society, accumulated labour is but a means to widen, to enrich, to promote the existence of the labourer

共産主義社会では、蓄積された労働は、労働者の存在を拡大し、富ませ、促進するための手段にすぎない

In Bourgeoisie society, therefore, the past dominates the present

したがって、ブルジョアジー社会では、過去が現在を支配している

in Communist society the present dominates the past

共産主義社会では、現在が過去を支配する

In Bourgeoisie society capital is independent and has individuality

ブルジョアジー社会では、資本は独立しており、個性がある

In Bourgeoisie society the living person is dependent and has no individuality

ブルジョアジー社会では、生きている人間は依存的であり、個性を持たない

And the abolition of this state of things is called by the Bourgeoisie, abolition of individuality and freedom!

そして、この状態の廃止は、ブルジョアジーによって、個性と自由の廃止と呼ばれています。

And it is rightly called the abolition of individuality and freedom!

そして、それはまさに個性と自由の廃止と呼ばれています。

Communism aims for the abolition of Bourgeoisie individuality

共産主義はブルジョアジーの個性の廃絶をめざす

Communism intends for the abolition of Bourgeoisie independence

共産主義はブルジョアジーの独立の廃止を意図している

Bourgeoisie freedom is undoubtedly what communism is aiming at

ブルジョアジーの自由は、疑いなく共産主義が目指しているものである

under the present Bourgeoisie conditions of production, freedom means free trade, free selling and buying

現在のブルジョアジーの生産条件のもとでは、自由とは自由貿易、自由な売買を意味する

But if selling and buying disappears, free selling and buying also disappears

しかし、売り買いがなくなると、自由な売りと買いもなくなります

"brave words" by the Bourgeoisie about free selling and buying only have meaning in a limited sense

ブルジョアジーによる自由な売買に関する「勇敢な言葉」は、限られた意味でしか意味を持たない

these words have meaning only in contrast with restricted selling and buying

これらの言葉は、制限された売りと買いとは対照的にのみ意味を持ちます

and these words have meaning only when applied to the fettered traders of the Middle Ages

そして、これらの言葉は、中世の束縛された商人に当てはめられたときにのみ意味を持つ

and that assumes these words even have meaning in a Bourgeoisie sense

そしてそれは、これらの言葉がブルジョアジー的な意味においてさえ意味を持つことを前提としている

but these words have no meaning when they're being used to oppose the Communistic abolition of buying and selling

しかし、これらの言葉は、共産主義による売買の廃止に反対するために使われているときは、何の意味もありません

the words have no meaning when they're being used to oppose the Bourgeoisie conditions of production being abolished

この言葉は、ブルジョアジーの生産条件が廃止されることに反対するために使われているときには、何の意味も持たない

and they have no meaning when they're being used to oppose the Bourgeoisie itself being abolished

そして、ブルジョアジーそのものが廃止されることに反対するために利用されているとき、それらは何の意味も持たない

You are horrified at our intending to do away with private property

あなた方は、私有財産を廃止しようとする私たちの意図にぞっとしています

But in your existing society, private property is already done away with for nine-tenths of the population

しかし、あなた方の既存の社会では、人口の9割の私有財産はすでに廃止されています

the existence of private property for the few is solely due to its non-existence in the hands of nine-tenths of the population

少数の者のための私有財産の存在は、ひとえに人口の10分の9の手中に私有財産が存在しないことによるものである

You reproach us, therefore, with intending to do away with a form of property

それゆえ、あなたは、財産の形態を廃止しようとしていると、私たちを非難します

but private property necessitates the non-existence of any

property for the immense majority of society

しかし、私有財産は、社会の圧倒的多数にとって、いかなる財産も存在しないことを要求する

In one word, you reproach us with intending to do away with your property

一言で言えば、あなたはあなたの財産を廃止するつもりで私たちを非難します

And it is precisely so; doing away with your Property is just what we intend

そして、それはまさにその通りです。あなたの財産を廃止することは、まさに私たちが意図していることです

From the moment when labour can no longer be converted into capital, money, or rent

労働が資本、貨幣、地代に転換できなくなった瞬間から

when labour can no longer be converted into a social power capable of being monopolised

労働がもはや独占可能な社会的権力に転換できなくなったとき

from the moment when individual property can no longer be transformed into Bourgeoisie property

個々の所有物がもはやブルジョアジーの所有物に転化できない瞬間から

from the moment when individual property can no longer be transformed into capital

個々の財産がもはや資本に転換できない瞬間から

from that moment, you say individuality vanishes

その瞬間から、個性が消えると言うのです

You must, therefore, confess that by "individual" you mean no other person than the Bourgeoisie

それゆえ、諸君は、「個人」とは、ブルジョアジー以外のいかなる者も意味しないことを告白しなければならない

you must confess it specifically refers to the middle-class owner of property

それはとりわけ特性の中流階級の所有者を示すことを告白しなければならない

This person must, indeed, be swept out of the way, and made impossible

この人は、実に、道から一掃され、不可能にされなければなりません

Communism deprives no man of the power to appropriate the products of society

共産主義は、社会の生産物を充当する力を誰からも奪わない

all that Communism does is to deprive him of the power to subjugate the labour of others by means of such appropriation

共産主義が行うことは、そのような横領によって他者の労働を征服する力を彼から奪うことだけである

It has been objected that upon the abolition of private property all work will cease

私有財産が廃止されれば、すべての仕事がなくなると反対されている

and it is then suggested that universal laziness will overtake us

そして、普遍的な怠惰が私たちを追い越すことが示唆されています

According to this, Bourgeoisie society ought long ago to have gone to the dogs through sheer idleness

これによれば、ブルジョアジー社会はとうの昔に、まったくの怠惰によって犬のところに行ってしまったはずである

because those of its members who work, acquire nothing

なぜなら、働いているそのメンバーのものは何も得られないからです

and those of its members who acquire anything, do not work

そして、そのメンバーのものは、何かを取得し、動作しません

The whole of this objection is but another expression of the tautology

この反論の全体は、トートロジーのもう一つの表現にすぎない

there can no longer be any wage-labour when there is no longer any capital

もはやいかなる資本も存在しないとき、いかなる賃労働も存在し得ない

there is no difference between material products and mental

products

物質的生産物と精神的生産物の間に違いはありません

communism proposes both of these are produced in the same way

共産主義は、これらの両方が同じ方法で生産されることを提案しています

but the objections against the Communistic modes of producing these are the same

しかし、これらを生産する共産主義的様式に対する異議は同じである

to the Bourgeoisie the disappearance of class property is the disappearance of production itself

ブルジョアジーにとって、階級的所有の消滅は、生産そのものの消滅である

so the disappearance of class culture is to him identical with the disappearance of all culture

したがって、階級文化の消滅は、彼にとってすべての文化の消滅と同じである

That culture, the loss of which he laments, is for the enormous majority a mere training to act as a machine

彼が嘆くその文化は、大多数の人々にとって、機械として振る舞うための単なる訓練に過ぎない

Communists very much intend to abolish the culture of Bourgeoisie property

共産主義者は、ブルジョアジーの財産文化を廃止する意図が強い

But don't wrangle with us so long as you apply the standard of your Bourgeoisie notions of freedom, culture, law, etc

しかし、自由、文化、法律などに関するブルジョアジーの観念の基準を適用する限り、私たちと論争しないでください

Your very ideas are but the outgrowth of the conditions of your Bourgeoisie production and Bourgeoisie property

諸君の観念そのものが、諸君のブルジョアジー生産とブルジョアジー諸財産の諸条件の産物にすぎない

just as your jurisprudence is but the will of your class made into a law for all

ちょうど、あなたがたの法学が、万人のための法律にされた

、あなたの階級の意志にすぎないように
the essential character and direction of this will are determined by the economical conditions your social class create
この意志の本質的な性格と方向性は、あなたの社会階級が作り出す経済的条件によって決定されます
The selfish misconception that induces you to transform social forms into eternal laws of nature and of reason
社会形態を自然と理性の永遠の法則に変えるようにあなたを誘導する利己的な誤解
the social forms springing from your present mode of production and form of property
あなたの現在の生産様式と財産形態から生じる社会的形態
historical relations that rise and disappear in the progress of production
生産の進行の中で浮き沈みする歴史的関係
this misconception you share with every ruling class that has preceded you
この誤解は、あなた方に先立つすべての支配階級と共有しています
What you see clearly in the case of ancient property, what you admit in the case of feudal property
古代の財産の場合にはっきりと見えるもの、封建的財産の場合に認めているもの
these things you are of course forbidden to admit in the case of your own Bourgeoisie form of property
これらの事柄は、もちろん、あなた自身のブルジョアジー的形態の所有の場合には、認めることを禁じられている
Abolition of the family! Even the most radical flare up at this infamous proposal of the Communists
家族廃止!最も過激な人々でさえ、共産主義者のこの悪名高い提案に燃え上がった
On what foundation is the present family, the Bourgeoisie family, based?
現在の家族、ブルジョアジー家は、どのような基盤の上に成り立っているのだろうか。
the foundation of the present family is based on capital and

private gain

現在の家族の基盤は、資本と私的利益に基づいています

In its completely developed form this family exists only among the Bourgeoisie

完全に発達した形態では、この家族はブルジョアジーの中にのみ存在します

this state of things finds its complement in the practical absence of the family among the proletarians

この状態は、プロレタリア階級のあいだに家族が事実上不在であることに、その補完を見いだす

this state of things can be found in public prostitution

このような状況は、公営売春にも見られます

The Bourgeoisie family will vanish as a matter of course when its complement vanishes

ブルジョアジー一家は、その補完物が消滅すれば、当然のように消滅する

and both of these will will vanish with the vanishing of capital

そして、この二つは、資本の消滅とともに消滅するであろう

Do you charge us with wanting to stop the exploitation of children by their parents?

親による子どもの搾取を止めたいと願っている私たちを責めますか?

To this crime we plead guilty

この犯罪に対して、私たちは有罪を認めます

But, you will say, we destroy the most hallowed of relations, when we replace home education by social education

しかし、家庭教育を社会教育に置き換えると、最も神聖な関係が破壊される、とあなたは言うでしょう

is your education not also social? And is it not determined by the social conditions under which you educate?

あなたがたの教育もまた社会的ではないのか。そして、それはあなたがたが教育する社会的条件によって決定されるのではないのか。

by the intervention, direct or indirect, of society, by means of schools, etc.

直接的または間接的な社会の介入、学校などによる介入によ

って。

The Communists have not invented the intervention of society in education

共産主義者は、教育への社会の介入を発明したのではない

they do but seek to alter the character of that intervention

彼らは、その介入の性格を変えようとしているに過ぎない

and they seek to rescue education from the influence of the ruling class

そして、彼らは支配階級の影響から教育を救おうとしています

The Bourgeoisie talk of the hallowed co-relation of parent and child

親と子の神聖な共関係についてのブルジョアジーの話

but this clap-trap about the family and education becomes all the more disgusting when we look at Modern Industry

しかし、家族と教育に関するこの拍手屏風は、現代の産業を見ると、いっそう嫌なものになります

all family ties among the proletarians are torn asunder by modern industry

プロレタリア階級の家族の絆は、近代産業によって引き裂かれている

their children are transformed into simple articles of commerce and instruments of labour

彼らの子供たちは、単純な商売道具や労働道具に変えられる

But you Communists would create a community of women, screams the whole Bourgeoisie in chorus

しかし、あなた方共産主義者は、女性の共同体をつくりだすだろう、とブルジョアジー全体が大合唱して叫ぶ

The Bourgeoisie sees in his wife a mere instrument of production

ブルジョアジーは、妻を単なる生産道具とみなしている

He hears that the instruments of production are to be exploited by all

彼は、生産の道具はすべての人によって搾取されるべきであると聞いています

and, naturally, he can come to no other conclusion than that the lot of being common to all will likewise fall to women

そして、当然のことながら、彼は、すべての人に共通する多くの存在が同様に女性に落ちるという結論にしか至り得ません

He has not even a suspicion that the real point is to do away with the status of women as mere instruments of production

彼は、本当の意味は、単なる生産道具としての女性の地位をなくすことにあるという疑念さえ持っていない

For the rest, nothing is more ridiculous than the virtuous indignation of our Bourgeoisie at the community of women

残りの人々にとって、女性の共同体に対するわがブルジョアジーの高潔な憤慨ほどばかげたものはない

they pretend it is to be openly and officially established by the Communists

彼らは、それが共産主義者によって公然と公式に確立されるふりをしている

The Communists have no need to introduce community of women, it has existed almost from time immemorial

共産主義者は女性のコミュニティを導入する必要はなく、それはほとんど太古の昔から存在していました

Our Bourgeoisie are not content with having the wives and daughters of their proletarians at their disposal

わがブルジョアジーは、プロレタリアの妻や娘を自由に使えることに満足していない

they take the greatest pleasure in seducing each other's wives

彼らはお互いの妻を誘惑することに最大の喜びを感じます

and that is not even to speak of common prostitutes

そして、それは一般的な売春婦について話すことではありません

Bourgeoisie marriage is in reality a system of wives in common

ブルジョアジーの結婚は、現実には共通の妻の制度である

then there is one thing that the Communists might possibly be reproached with

そして、共産主義者が非難されるかもしれないことが一つある

they desire to introduce an openly legalised community of

women
彼らは、公然と合法化された女性のコミュニティを導入する
ことを望んでいます
rather than a hypocritically concealed community of women
偽善的に隠された女性のコミュニティではなく
the community of women springing from the system of
production
生産システムから生まれた女性の共同体
abolish the system of production, and you abolish the
community of women
生産制度を廃止し、女性の共同体を廃止せよ
both public prostitution is abolished, and private
prostitution
公営売春も私娼も廃止
The Communists are further more reproached with desiring
to abolish countries and nationality
共産主義者は、国家と民族を廃止したいと願うことで、さら
に非難される
The working men have no country, so we cannot take from
them what they have not got
労働者には国がないので、彼らが持っていないものを彼らか
ら奪うことはできません
the proletariat must first of all acquire political supremacy
プロレタリアートは、まず第一に政治的優越性を獲得しなけ
ればならない
the proletariat must rise to be the leading class of the nation
プロレタリアートは、国家の指導的階級にならなければなら
ない
the proletariat must constitute itself the nation
プロレタリアートは、それ自身を国家として構成しなければ
ならない
it is, so far, itself national, though not in the Bourgeoisie
sense of the word
それは、これまでのところ、それ自体が国民的であるが、ブ
ルジョアジー的な意味でのものではない
National differences and antagonisms between peoples are
daily more and more vanishing

民族間の国家間の相違と敵対関係は、日々ますます消滅して
います

owing to the development of the Bourgeoisie, to freedom of
commerce, to the world-market
ブルジョアジーの発展、商業の自由、世界市場の発展のため
に

to uniformity in the mode of production and in the
conditions of life corresponding thereto
生産様式とそれに対応する生活条件の均一性

The supremacy of the proletariat will cause them to vanish
still faster
プロレタリアートの優越性は、彼らをいっそう早く消滅させ
るだろう

United action, of the leading civilised countries at least, is
one of the first conditions for the emancipation of the
proletariat
少なくとも主要な文明国の団結した行動は、プロレタリアー
ト解放の第一条件の一つである

In proportion as the exploitation of one individual by
another is put an end to, the exploitation of one nation by
another will also be put an end to
ある個人が別の個人によって搾取されることに比例して、あ
る国が別の国によって搾取されることも、

In proportion as the antagonism between classes within the
nation vanishes, the hostility of one nation to another will
come to an end
国内の階級間の対立が消えるのに比例して、ある民族から別
の民族への敵意は終わりを告げるであろう

The charges against Communism made from a religious, a
philosophical, and, generally, from an ideological
standpoint, are not deserving of serious examination
宗教的、哲学的、そして一般的にはイデオロギー的見地から
なされた共産主義に対する非難は、真剣に検討するに値しな
い

Does it require deep intuition to comprehend that man's
ideas, views and conceptions changes with every change in
the conditions of his material existence?

人間の考え、見解、概念が、物質的存在の状態が変化するたびに変化するということを理解するには、深い直観が必要ですか?

is it not obvious that man's consciousness changes when his social relations and his social life changes?

人間の社会関係や社会生活が変われば、人間の意識も変わるのは明らかではないでしょうか。

What else does the history of ideas prove, than that intellectual production changes its character in proportion as material production is changed?

思想史が証明しているのは、知的生産が物質的生産が変化すれば、それに比例してその性格も変化するということである。

The ruling ideas of each age have ever been the ideas of its ruling class

各時代の支配思想は、つねに支配階級の思想であった

When people speak of ideas that revolutionise society, they do but express one fact

人々が社会に革命を起こすアイデアについて語るとき、彼らは一つの事実を表現しているに過ぎない

within the old society, the elements of a new one have been created

古い社会の中で、新しい社会の要素が創造されました

and that the dissolution of the old ideas keeps even pace with the dissolution of the old conditions of existence

そして、古い考えの解体は、古い存在条件の解消と歩調を合わせている

When the ancient world was in its last throes, the ancient religions were overcome by Christianity

古代世界が最後の苦しみにあったとき、古代の宗教はキリスト教に打ち負かされました

When Christian ideas succumbed in the 18th century to rationalist ideas, feudal society fought its death battle with the then revolutionary Bourgeoisie

18世紀にキリスト教の思想が合理主義の思想に屈したとき、封建社会は当時の革命的ブルジョアジーと死闘を繰り広げた

The ideas of religious liberty and freedom of conscience

merely gave expression to the sway of free competition within the domain of knowledge

信教の自由と良心の自由という考えは、知識の領域における自由競争の影響力を表現したに過ぎない

"Undoubtedly," it will be said, "religious, moral, philosophical and juridical ideas have been modified in the course of historical development"

「疑いなく」と言われるだろう、「宗教的、道徳的、哲学的、法的な考えは、歴史的発展の過程で修正されてきた」

"But religion, morality philosophy, political science, and law, constantly survived this change"

「しかし、宗教、道徳哲学、政治学、法学は、常にこの変化を生き延びてきた」

"There are also eternal truths, such as Freedom, Justice, etc"

「自由、正義などの永遠の真理もあります」

"these eternal truths are common to all states of society"

「これらの永遠の真理は、社会のすべての状態に共通しています」

"But Communism abolishes eternal truths, it abolishes all religion, and all morality"

「しかし、共産主義は永遠の真理を廃止し、すべての宗教とすべての道徳を廃止する」

"it does this instead of constituting them on a new basis"

「新しい基準でそれらを構成する代わりに、これを行う」

"it therefore acts in contradiction to all past historical experience"

「それゆえ、それは過去のすべての歴史的経験と矛盾して行動する」

What does this accusation reduce itself to?

この非難は何に還元されるのでしょうか?

The history of all past society has consisted in the development of class antagonisms

過去のすべての社会の歴史は、階級対立の発展から成り立ってきた

antagonisms that assumed different forms at different epochs

異なる時代に異なる形態をとった拮抗

But whatever form they may have taken, one fact is common to all past ages
しかし、彼らがどのような形をとったにせよ、過去のすべての時代に共通する事実が1つあります

the exploitation of one part of society by the other
社会のある部分が他の部分を搾取すること

No wonder, then, that the social consciousness of past ages moves within certain common forms, or general ideas
それゆえ、過去の時代の社会意識が、ある種の共通の形態、あるいは一般的な観念の中で動いているのも不思議ではない

(and that is despite all the multiplicity and variety it displays)
(そしてそれは、それが表示するすべての多様性と多様性にもかかわらずです)

and these cannot completely vanish except with the total disappearance of class antagonisms
そして、これらは、階級的対立の完全な消滅なしには、完全に消滅することはできない

The Communist revolution is the most radical rupture with traditional property relations
共産主義革命は、伝統的な財産関係の最も根本的な断絶である

no wonder that its development involves the most radical rupture with traditional ideas
その発展が伝統的な考えとの最も根本的な断絶を伴うのも不思議ではありません

But let us have done with the Bourgeoisie objections to Communism
しかし、共産主義に対するブルジョアジーの異議申し立てはこれで終わりにしよう

We have seen above the first step in the revolution by the working class
われわれは以上、労働者階級による革命の第一段階を見た

proletariat has to be raised to the position of ruling, to win the battle of democracy
プロレタリアートは、民主主義の戦いに勝つために、支配的な地位に引き上げられなければならない

The proletariat will use its political supremacy to wrest, by degrees, all capital from the Bourgeoisie
プロレタリアートは、その政治的優越性を利用して、ブルジョアジーからすべての資本を少しずつ奪い取るであろう

it will centralise all instruments of production in the hands of the State
それは、すべての生産手段を国家の手に集中させるであろう

in other words, the proletariat organised as the ruling class
言い換えれば、プロレタリアートは支配階級として組織された

and it will increase the total of productive forces as rapidly as possible
そして、生産力の総量を可能な限り急速に増やすであろう

Of course, in the beginning, this cannot be effected except by means of despotic inroads on the rights of property
もちろん、初めのうちは、これは専制的な財産権の侵害によってのみ実現することはできない

and it has to be achieved on the conditions of Bourgeoisie production
そして、それはブルジョアジー生産の条件で達成されなければならない

it is achieved by means of measures, therefore, which appear economically insufficient and untenable
したがって、それは経済的に不十分で維持できないように見える手段によって達成されます

but these means, in the course of the movement, outstrip themselves
しかし、これらの手段は、運動の過程で、それ自体を凌駕します

they necessitate further inroads upon the old social order
それらは、古い社会秩序にさらに侵入することを必要とする

and they are unavoidable as a means of entirely revolutionising the mode of production
そして、それらは生産様式を全面的に革命する手段として避けられない

These measures will of course be different in different countries

もちろん、これらの措置は国によって異なります

Nevertheless in the most advanced countries, the following will be pretty generally applicable

それにもかかわらず、最も先進国では、以下がかなり一般的に適用されます

1. Abolition of property in land and application of all rents of land to public purposes.

1.

土地の財産を廃止し、すべての土地の賃貸料を公共目的に充てること。

2. A heavy progressive or graduated income tax.

2.重い累進所得税または累進所得税。

3. Abolition of all right of inheritance.

3. 相続権の廃止

4. Confiscation of the property of all emigrants and rebels.

4.すべての移民と反逆者の財産の没収。

5. Centralisation of credit in the hands of the State, by means of a national bank with State capital and an exclusive monopoly.

5.

国家資本と独占的独占を有する国立銀行による国家の手中への信用の集中化。

6. Centralisation of the means of communication and transport in the hands of the State.

6. 通信手段と輸送手段を国家の手に集中化すること。

7. Extension of factories and instruments of production owned by the State

7. 国家所有の工場及び生産手段の拡張

the bringing into cultivation of waste-lands, and the improvement of the soil generally in accordance with a common plan.

荒れ地の耕作と、一般的な計画に従った土壌の改良。

8. Equal liability of all to labour

8. 労働に対するすべての人の平等な責任

Establishment of industrial armies, especially for agriculture.

特に農業のための産業軍隊の設立。

9. Combination of agriculture with manufacturing industries
9. 農業と製造業の融合

gradual abolition of the distinction between town and country, by a more equable distribution of the population over the country.
町と田舎の区別を徐々に廃止し、全国の人口のより公平な分配によって。

10. Free education for all children in public schools.
10.公立学校のすべての子供のための無料の教育。

Abolition of children's factory labour in its present form
現在の形態の児童工場労働の廃止

Combination of education with industrial production
教育と工業生産の融合

When, in the course of development, class distinctions have disappeared
発展の過程で、階級の区別がなくなったとき

and when all production has been concentrated in the hands of a vast association of the whole nation
そして、すべての生産が全国民の広大な協会の手に集中したとき

then the public power will lose its political character
そうなれば、公権力は政治的性格を失うだろう

Political power, properly so called, is merely the organised power of one class for oppressing another
政治権力とは、正しくはそう呼ばれているが、ある階級が他の階級を抑圧するための組織化された権力にすぎない

If the proletariat during its contest with the Bourgeoisie is compelled, by the force of circumstances, to organise itself as a class
もしプロレタリアートがブルジョアジーとの争いの最中に、状況の力によって階級として組織せざるを得ないならば、

if, by means of a revolution, it makes itself the ruling class
もし、革命によって、自らを支配階級にするならば

and, as such, it sweeps away by force the old conditions of production
そして、そのようにして、それは力ずくで古い生産条件を一掃します

then it will, along with these conditions, have swept away
the conditions for the existence of class antagonisms and of
classes generally

そうすれば、これらの条件とともに、階級対立と階級一般の
存在条件を一掃することになる

and will thereby have abolished its own supremacy as a
class.

そして、それによって階級としての自己の優越性を廃止する
であろう。

In place of the old Bourgeoisie society, with its classes and
class antagonisms, we shall have an association

階級と階級対立をもった古いブルジョアジー社会にかわって
、われわれは結社をもつであろう

an association in which the free development of each is the
condition for the free development of all

各々の自由な発展が、すべての人の自由な発展の条件である
連合

Reactionary Socialism
反動的な社会主義

a) Feudal Socialism
a) 封建的社会主義

the aristocracies of France and England had a unique historical position
フランスとイギリスの貴族階級は、独自の歴史的位置を占めていました

it became their vocation to write pamphlets against modern Bourgeoisie society
近代ブルジョアジー社会に反対するパンフレットを書くことが彼らの職業となった

In the French revolution of July 1830, and in the English reform agitation
1830年7月のフランス革命とイギリスの改革扇動

these aristocracies again succumbed to the hateful upstart
これらの貴族階級は、再び憎むべき成り上がり者に屈した

Thenceforth, a serious political contest was altogether out of the question
それ以来、真剣な政治闘争は全く問題外となった

All that remained possible was literary battle, not an actual battle
残されたのは文学的な戦いだけで、実際の戦いではなかった

But even in the domain of literature the old cries of the restoration period had become impossible
しかし、文学の領域においてさえ、王政復古期の古い叫びは不可能になっていた

In order to arouse sympathy, the aristocracy were obliged to lose sight, apparently, of their own interests
同情を呼び起こすために、貴族階級は、明らかに、自分たちの利益を見失わざるを得なかった

and they were obliged to formulate their indictment against the Bourgeoisie in the interest of the exploited working class
そして彼らは、搾取された労働者階級の利益のために、ブルジョアジーに対する告発を策定する義務を負った

Thus the aristocracy took their revenge by singing lampoons on their new master

こうして貴族たちは、新しい主人に悪口を歌うことで復讐を果たした

and they took their revenge by whispering in his ears sinister prophecies of coming catastrophe

そして、彼らは彼の耳元で来るべき破局の不吉な予言をささやくことによって復讐を果たした

In this way arose Feudal Socialism: half lamentation, half lampoon

このようにして封建的社会主義が生まれた:半分は嘆き、半分は風刺

it rung as half echo of the past, and projected half menace of the future

それは半分は過去の反響のように鳴り響き、半分は未来の脅威を映し出していた

at times, by its bitter, witty and incisive criticism, it struck the Bourgeoisie to the very heart's core

時には、その辛辣で機知に富んだ鋭い批評によって、ブルジョアジーの心を揺さぶった

but it was always ludicrous in its effect, through total incapacity to comprehend the march of modern history

しかし、それは、近代史の行進を理解する完全な無能力によって、その効果において常に滑稽なものであった

The aristocracy, in order to rally the people to them, waved the proletarian alms-bag in front for a banner

貴族階級は、民衆を彼らに結集させるために、プロレタリアの施し袋を前に振って旗を掲げた

But the people, so often as it joined them, saw on their hindquarters the old feudal coats of arms

しかし、民衆は、しばしば彼らに加わると、彼らの後ろに古い封建的な紋章を見た

and they deserted with loud and irreverent laughter

そして、彼らは大声で不遜な笑い声をあげて逃げ出した

One section of the French Legitimists and "Young England" exhibited this spectacle

フランスの正統派と「若いイングランド」の一部は、この光

景を呈した

the feudalists pointed out that their mode of exploitation
was different to that of the Bourgeoisie
封建主義者は、彼らの搾取の様式がブルジョアジーのそれと
は異なることを指摘した

the feudalists forget that they exploited under circumstances
and conditions that were quite different
封建主義者は、まったく異なる状況と条件の下で搾取したこ
とを忘れています

and they didn't notice such methods of exploitation are now
antiquated
そして、彼らはそのような搾取の方法が今や時代遅れである
ことに気づかなかったのです

they showed that, under their rule, the modern proletariat
never existed
彼らは、彼らの支配下では、現代のプロレタリアートは決し
て存在しなかったことを示した

but they forget that the modern Bourgeoisie is the necessary
offspring of their own form of society
しかし、彼らは、現代のブルジョアジーが、彼ら自身の社会
形態の必然的な子孫であることを忘れている

For the rest, they hardly conceal the reactionary character of
their criticism
それ以外の部分については、彼らは批判の反動的な性格をほ
とんど隠そうとしない

their chief accusation against the Bourgeoisie amounts to the
following
ブルジョアジーに対する彼らの主な非難は、次のようになる

under the Bourgeoisie regime a social class is being
developed
ブルジョアジー体制のもとで、社会階級が発展しつつある

this social class is destined to cut up root and branch the old
order of society
この社会階級は、社会の古い秩序を根こそぎ切り裂き、枝分
かれさせる運命にある

What they upbraid the Bourgeoisie with is not so much that
it creates a proletariat

彼らがブルジョアジーを褒め称えるのは、それがプロレタリアートを生み出すことではない

what they upbraid the Bourgeoisie with is moreso that it creates a revolutionary proletariat

かれらがブルジョアジーをたたきつけるのは、革命的プロレタリアートをつくりだすということである

In political practice, therefore, they join in all coercive measures against the working class

それゆえ、政治的実践において、彼らは労働者階級に対するあらゆる強制的措置に加わるのである

and in ordinary life, despite their highfalutin phrases, they stoop to pick up the golden apples dropped from the tree of industry

そして、普段の生活では、高尚なフレーズにもかかわらず、産業の木から落ちた金のリンゴを拾うために身をかがめます

and they barter truth, love, and honour for commerce in wool, beetroot-sugar, and potato spirits

そして、彼らは真実、愛、名誉を羊毛、甜菜糖、ジャガイモの蒸留酒の商売と交換する

As the parson has ever gone hand in hand with the landlord, so has Clerical Socialism with Feudal Socialism

牧師が地主と手を携えて歩んできたように、聖職者社会主義と封建的社会主義もそうであった

Nothing is easier than to give Christian asceticism a Socialist tinge

キリスト教の禁欲主義に社会主義的な色合いを与えることほど簡単なことはありません

Has not Christianity declaimed against private property, against marriage, against the State?

キリスト教は、私有財産、結婚、国家に反対したのではないだろうか。

Has Christianity not preached in the place of these, charity and poverty?

キリスト教は、これらの慈善と貧困の代わりに説教したのではないだろうか。

Does Christianity not preach celibacy and mortification of the flesh, monastic life and Mother Church?

キリスト教は、肉の独身と苦行、修道生活、母なる教会を説いているのではないでしょうか。

Christian Socialism is but the holy water with which the priest consecrates the heart-burnings of the aristocrat

キリスト教社会主義は、聖職者が貴族の心の燃え上がりを聖別するための聖水にすぎない

b) Petty-Bourgeois Socialism
b) 小ブルジョア社会主義

The feudal aristocracy was not the only class that was ruined by the Bourgeoisie
ブルジョアジーによって破滅させられた階級は封建貴族だけではなかった

it was not the only class whose conditions of existence pined and perished in the atmosphere of modern Bourgeoisie society
近代ブルジョアジー社会の雰囲気の中で生存条件が固まり、消滅した階級は、それだけではなかった

The medieval burgesses and the small peasant proprietors were the precursors of the modern Bourgeoisie
中世の領主と小農民は、近代ブルジョアジーの先駆者であった

In those countries which are but little developed, industrially and commercially, these two classes still vegetate side by side
工業的にも商業的にもほとんど発展していない国々では、この2つの階級がいまだに隣り合って植生している

and in the meantime the Bourgeoisie rise up next to them: industrially, commercially, and politically
そしてその間、ブルジョアジーは、産業的にも、商業的にも、政治的にも、彼らの隣で立ち上がる

In countries where modern civilisation has become fully developed, a new class of petty Bourgeoisie has been formed
近代文明が十分に発達した国々では、新しい階級の小ブルジョアジーが形成された

this new social class fluctuates between proletariat and Bourgeoisie
この新しい社会階級は、プロレタリアートとブルジョアジーの間で揺れ動く

and it is ever renewing itself as a supplementary part of Bourgeoisie society
そして、それはブルジョアジー社会の補助的な部分として絶えず更新されつつある

The individual members of this class, however, are being constantly hurled down into the proletariat

しかし、この階級の個々の構成員は、絶えずプロレタリアートに投げ落とされている

they are sucked up by the proletariat through the action of competition

彼らは競争の作用によってプロレタリアートに吸い上げられる

as modern industry develops they even see the moment approaching when they will completely disappear as an independent section of modern society

近代産業が発展するにつれて、彼らは現代社会の独立した部分として完全に消滅する瞬間が近づいているとさえ見ています

they will be replaced, in manufactures, agriculture and commerce, by overlookers, bailiffs and shopmen

彼らは、製造業、農業、商業において、監督者、廷吏、商店員に取って代わられるでしょう

In countries like France, where the peasants constitute far more than half of the population

フランスのような国では、農民が人口の半分以上を占めています

it was natural that there there are writers who sided with the proletariat against the Bourgeoisie

ブルジョアジーに対してプロレタリアートに味方した作家がいるのは当然のことだった

in their criticism of the Bourgeoisie regime they used the standard of the peasant and petty Bourgeoisie

ブルジョアジー体制を批判するにあたって、かれらは農民と小ブルジョアジーの基準を利用した

and from the standpoint of these intermediate classes they take up the cudgels for the working class

そして、これらの中間階級の立場から、彼らは労働者階級のために棍棒を取り上げます

Thus arose petty-Bourgeoisie Socialism, of which Sismondi was the head of this school, not only in France but also in England

こうして小ブルジョアジー社会主義が勃発し、シスモンディ
はフランスだけでなくイギリスでもこの学派の長であった

This school of Socialism dissected with great acuteness the contradictions in the conditions of modern production

この社会主義学派は、近代的生産条件の矛盾を非常に鋭く解剖した

This school laid bare the hypocritical apologies of economists

この学派は、経済学者の偽善的な謝罪を暴露した

This school proved, incontrovertibly, the disastrous effects of machinery and division of labour

この学校は、議論の余地なく、機械と分業の悲惨な影響を証明しました

it proved the concentration of capital and land in a few hands

それは、資本と土地が少数の手に集中していることを証明した

it proved how overproduction leads to Bourgeoisie crises

それは、過剰生産がいかにブルジョアジーの危機につながるかを証明した

it pointed out the inevitable ruin of the petty Bourgeoisie and peasant

それは、小ブルジョアジーと農民の必然的な破滅を指摘した

the misery of the proletariat, the anarchy in production, the crying inequalities in the distribution of wealth

プロレタリアートの悲惨さ、生産の無政府状態、富の分配における泣き叫ぶような不平等

it showed how the system of production leads the industrial war of extermination between nations

それは、生産システムが国家間の絶滅という産業戦争をどのようにリードしているかを示しました

the dissolution of old moral bonds, of the old family relations, of the old nationalities

古い道徳的絆、古い家族関係、古い民族の解体

In its positive aims, however, this form of Socialism aspires to achieve one of two things

しかし、この形態の社会主義は、その肯定的な目的において

、次の2つのことのうちの1つを達成することを熱望している

either it aims to restore the old means of production and of exchange

それは、古い生産手段と交換手段の復活を目指すかのどちらかである

and with the old means of production it would restore the old property relations, and the old society

そして、古い生産手段によって、古い所有関係と古い社会を回復させるだろう

or it aims to cramp the modern means of production and exchange into the old framework of the property relations

あるいは、近代的な生産手段と交換手段を、所有関係の古い枠組みに押し込めることをめざしている

In either case, it is both reactionary and Utopian

いずれにせよ、それは反動的であり、ユートピア的である

Its last words are: corporate guilds for manufacture, patriarchal relations in agriculture

その最後の言葉は、製造のための企業ギルド、農業における家父長制の関係です

Ultimately, when stubborn historical facts had dispersed all intoxicating effects of self-deception

究極的には、頑固な歴史的事実が自己欺瞞の陶酔効果をすべて分散させたとき

this form of Socialism ended in a miserable fit of pity

この形態の社会主義は、惨めな哀れみの発作に終わった

c) German, or "True," Socialism
c) ドイツ、または「真の」社会主義

The Socialist and Communist literature of France originated under the pressure of a Bourgeoisie in power
フランスの社会主義と共産主義の文学は、権力を握ったブルジョアジーの圧力の下で生まれた

and this literature was the expression of the struggle against this power
そして、この文学は、この権力に対する闘争の表現であった

it was introduced into Germany at a time when the Bourgeoisie had just begun its contest with feudal absolutism
それは、ブルジョアジーが封建的絶対主義との競争を始めたばかりの時期にドイツに導入されました

German philosophers, would-be philosophers, and beaux esprits, eagerly seized on this literature
ドイツの哲学者、哲学者志望者、そして美女のエスプリは、この文献を熱心につかみました

but they forgot that the writings immigrated from France into Germany without bringing the French social conditions along
しかし、彼らは、この著作がフランスの社会状況をもたらすことなく、フランスからドイツに移住したことを忘れていた

In contact with German social conditions, this French literature lost all its immediate practical significance
ドイツの社会状況と接触するうちに、このフランス文学は直接的な実践的意義を失った

and the Communist literature of France assumed a purely literary aspect in German academic circles
フランスの共産主義文学は、ドイツの学界では純粋に文学的な側面を帯びていた

Thus, the demands of the first French Revolution were nothing more than the demands of "Practical Reason"
したがって、第一次フランス革命の要求は「実践理性」の要求にすぎなかった

and the utterance of the will of the revolutionary French

Bourgeoisie signified in their eyes the law of pure Will

そして、革命的なフランス・ブルジョアジーの意志の発声は、彼らの目には純粋な意志の法則を意味していた

it signified Will as it was bound to be; of true human Will generally

それは、あるべき意志を意味していた。真の人間の意志一般の

The world of the German literati consisted solely in bringing the new French ideas into harmony with their ancient philosophical conscience

ドイツの文学者の世界は、もっぱら新しいフランスの思想を彼らの古代の哲学的良心と調和させることにあった

or rather, they annexed the French ideas without deserting their own philosophic point of view

というか、彼らは自らの哲学的観点を捨てることなく、フランスの思想を併合した

This annexation took place in the same way in which a foreign language is appropriated, namely, by translation

この併合は、外国語が流用されるのと同じ方法、つまり翻訳によって行われました

It is well known how the monks wrote silly lives of Catholic Saints over manuscripts

修道士たちがカトリックの聖人の愚かな人生を写本の上に書いたことはよく知られています

the manuscripts on which the classical works of ancient heathendom had been written

古代異教徒の古典作品が書かれた写本

The German literati reversed this process with the profane French literature

ドイツの文学者は、この過程を冒涜的なフランス文学で逆転させた

They wrote their philosophical nonsense beneath the French original

彼らはフランス語の原文の下に哲学的なナンセンスを書いた

For instance, beneath the French criticism of the economic functions of money, they wrote "Alienation of Humanity"

例えば、貨幣の経済的機能に対するフランスの批判の下に、

彼らは「人類の疎外」を書いた

beneath the French criticism of the Bourgeoisie State they wrote "dethronement of the Category of the General"

ブルジョアジー国家に対するフランスの批判の下に、彼らは「将軍のカテゴリーの退位」を書いた

The introduction of these philosophical phrases at the back of the French historical criticisms they dubbed:

これらの哲学的フレーズの導入は、彼らがダビングしたフランスの歴史批評の背後にあります。

"Philosophy of Action," "True Socialism," "German Science of Socialism," "Philosophical Foundation of Socialism," and so on

「行動の哲学」「真の社会主義」「ドイツ社会主義の科学」「社会主義の哲学的基礎」など

The French Socialist and Communist literature was thus completely emasculated

こうして、フランスの社会主義と共産主義の文学は完全に去勢された

in the hands of the German philosophers it ceased to express the struggle of one class with the other

ドイツの哲学者の手によって、それはある階級と他の階級との闘争を表現することをやめた

and so the German philosophers felt conscious of having overcome "French one-sidedness"

こうして、ドイツの哲学者たちは「フランスの一面性」を克服したことを意識したのである

it did not have to represent true requirements, rather, it represented requirements of truth

それは真の要求を表す必要はなく、むしろ真理の要求を表していたのです

there was no interest in the proletariat, rather, there was interest in Human Nature

プロレタリアートには関心がなく、むしろ人間性に関心があった

the interest was in Man in general, who belongs to no class, and has no reality

その関心は、いかなる階級にも属さず、実在性をもたない人

間一般に向けられていた

a man who exists only in the misty realm of philosophical fantasy

哲学的幻想の霧の領域にしか存在しない男

but eventually this schoolboy German Socialism also lost its pedantic innocence

しかし、やがてこの小学生ドイツ社会主義もまた、その衒学的な無邪気さを失った

the German Bourgeoisie, and especially the Prussian Bourgeoisie fought against feudal aristocracy

ドイツのブルジョアジー、特にプロイセンのブルジョアジーは封建貴族と戦った

the absolute monarchy of Germany and Prussia was also being faught against

ドイツとプロイセンの絶対君主制もまた、

and in turn, the literature of the liberal movement also became more earnest

そして、リベラルな運動の文学もより真剣になっていった

Germany's long wished-for opportunity for "true" Socialism was offered

ドイツが長い間望んでいた「真の」社会主義の機会がもたらされた

the opportunity of confronting the political movement with the Socialist demands

社会主義の要求と政治運動に立ち向かう機会

the opportunity of hurling the traditional anathemas against liberalism

リベラリズムに対する伝統的な忌み嫌われる機会

the opportunity to attack representative government and Bourgeoisie competition

代議制政府とブルジョアジーの競争を攻撃する機会

Bourgeoisie freedom of the press, Bourgeoisie legislation, Bourgeoisie liberty and equality

ブルジョアジーの報道の自由、ブルジョアジーの立法、ブルジョアジーの自由と平等

all of these could now be critiqued in the real world, rather than in fantasy

これらはすべて、ファンタジーではなく、現実の世界で批評できるようになりました

feudal aristocracy and absolute monarchy had long preached to the masses

封建貴族と絶対君主制は長い間大衆に説教していた

"the working man has nothing to lose, and he has everything to gain"

「労働者は失うものは何もなく、得るものはすべて持っている」

the Bourgeoisie movement also offered a chance to confront these platitudes

ブルジョアジー運動もまた、こうした決まり文句に立ち向かう機会を与えた

the French criticism presupposed the existence of modern Bourgeoisie society

フランス批判は、近代ブルジョアジー社会の存在を前提としていた

Bourgeoisie economic conditions of existence and Bourgeoisie political constitution

ブルジョアジーの存在条件とブルジョアジーの政治体質

the very things whose attainment was the object of the pending struggle in Germany

その達成がドイツにおける差し迫った闘争の対象であったまさにその事柄

Germany's silly echo of socialism abandoned these goals just in the nick of time

ドイツの社会主義の愚かな反響は、これらの目標を間一髪で放棄した

the absolute governments had their following of parsons, professors, country squires and officials

絶対政府には、牧師、教授、田舎の大地主、役人がいました

the government of the time met the German working-class risings with floggings and bullets

当時の政府は、ドイツの労働者階級の蜂起に鞭打ちと銃弾で立ち向かった

for them this socialism served as a welcome scarecrow against the threatening Bourgeoisie

彼らにとって、この社会主義は、ブルジョアジーの脅威に対する歓迎すべきかかしとして機能した

and the German government was able to offer a sweet dessert after the bitter pills it handed out

そして、ドイツ政府は、苦い薬を配った後、甘いデザートを提供することができました

this "True" Socialism thus served the governments as a weapon for fighting the German Bourgeoisie

この「真の」社会主義は、こうして、ドイツ・ブルジョアジーと戦うための武器として、政府に役立ったのである

and, at the same time, it directly represented a reactionary interest; that of the German Philistines

そして同時に、それは直接的に反動的な利害を代表していた。ドイツ・ペリシテ人のそれ

In Germany the petty Bourgeoisie class is the real social basis of the existing state of things

ドイツでは、小ブルジョア階級が現存する諸事態の真の社会的基盤である

a relique of the sixteenth century that has constantly been cropping up under various forms

16世紀の遺物は、さまざまな形で絶えず出現しています

To preserve this class is to preserve the existing state of things in Germany

この階級を維持することは、ドイツの現状を維持することである

The industrial and political supremacy of the Bourgeoisie threatens the petty Bourgeoisie with certain destruction

ブルジョアジーの産業的・政治的優越性は、小ブルジョアジーを一定の破壊で脅かす

on the one hand, it threatens to destroy the petty Bourgeoisie through the concentration of capital

一方では、資本の集中によって小ブルジョアジーを破壊する恐れがある

on the other hand, the Bourgeoisie threatens to destroy it through the rise of a revolutionary proletariat

他方、ブルジョアジーは、革命的プロレタリアートの勃興によって、ブルジョアジーを破壊すると脅す

"True" Socialism appeared to kill these two birds with one stone. It spread like an epidemic

「真の」社会主義は、この二羽の鳥を一石二鳥に仕留めるように見えた。伝染病のように広がった

The robe of speculative cobwebs, embroidered with flowers of rhetoric, steeped in the dew of sickly sentiment

レトリックの花が刺繍された思索的な蜘蛛の巣のローブは、病的な感傷の露に染まっていた

this transcendental robe in which the German Socialists wrapped their sorry "eternal truths"

ドイツ社会主義者が哀れな「永遠の真理」を包んだこの超越的なローブ

all skin and bone, served to wonderfully increase the sale of their goods amongst such a public

すべての皮と骨は、そのような公衆の間で彼らの商品の売り上げを素晴らしく増やすのに役立ちました

And on its part, German Socialism recognised, more and more, its own calling

そして、ドイツ社会主義は、自らの使命をますます認識していった

it was called to be the bombastic representative of the petty-Bourgeoisie Philistine

それは、小ブルジョアジーのペリシテ人の大げさな代表として召された

It proclaimed the German nation to be the model nation, and German petty Philistine the model man

それは、ドイツ国民を模範国家とし、ドイツの小ペリシテ人を模範とすると宣言した

To every villainous meanness of this model man it gave a hidden, higher, Socialistic interpretation

この模範的な男のあらゆる極悪非道な卑劣さに、それは隠された、より高い、社会主義的な解釈を与えた

this higher, Socialistic interpretation was the exact contrary of its real character

このより高尚な社会主義的解釈は、その真の性格とは正反対であった

It went to the extreme length of directly opposing the

"brutally destructive" tendency of Communism
それは、共産主義の「残忍な破壊的」傾向に真っ向から反対するという極端な長さにまで踏み込んだ
and it proclaimed its supreme and impartial contempt of all class struggles
そして、すべての階級闘争に対する最高かつ公平な軽蔑を宣言した
With very few exceptions, all the so-called Socialist and Communist publications that now (1847) circulate in Germany belong to the domain of this foul and enervating literature
ごく少数の例外を除いて、現在(1847年)ドイツで流通しているすべてのいわゆる社会主義および共産主義の出版物は、この汚らわしく活力に満ちた文学の領域に属しています

Conservative Socialism, or Bourgeoisie Socialism
保守社会主義、あるいはブルジョアジー社会主義

A part of the Bourgeoisie is desirous of redressing social grievances
ブルジョアジーの一部は、社会的不満を是正することを望んでいる

in order to secure the continued existence of Bourgeoisie society
ブルジョアジー社会の存続を保障するために

To this section belong economists, philanthropists, humanitarians
このセクションには、経済学者、慈善家、人道主義者が属しています

improvers of the condition of the working class and organisers of charity
労働者階級の状態の改善者と慈善活動の組織者

members of societies for the prevention of cruelty to animals
動物虐待防止協会会員

temperance fanatics, hole-and-corner reformers of every imaginable kind
禁酒狂信者、ありとあらゆる種類の穴と角の改革者

This form of Socialism has, moreover, been worked out into complete systems
さらに、この形態の社会主義は、完全なシステムとして作り上げられた

We may cite Proudhon's "Philosophie de la Misère" as an example of this form
プルードンの「ミゼール哲学」をその例として挙げてみましょう

The Socialistic Bourgeoisie want all the advantages of modern social conditions
社会主義ブルジョアジーは、近代的社会条件のあらゆる利点を欲しがっている

but the Socialistic Bourgeoisie don't necessarily want the resulting struggles and dangers
しかし、社会主義ブルジョアジーは、必ずしも結果として生

じる闘争と危険を望んでいるわけではない

They desire the existing state of society, minus its
revolutionary and disintegrating elements

彼らは、革命的・崩壊的要素を差し引いた、現存する社会状
態を望んでいる

in other words, they wish for a Bourgeoisie without a
proletariat

言い換えれば、彼らはプロレタリアートのいないブルジョア
ジーを望んでいるのである

The Bourgeoisie naturally conceives the world in which it is
supreme to be the best

ブルジョアジーは、自分が最高である世界を自然に思い描く

and Bourgeoisie Socialism develops this comfortable
conception into various more or less complete systems

そして、ブルジョアジー社会主義は、この快適な概念を、多
かれ少なかれ完全なさまざまな体系に発展させる

they would very much like the proletariat to march
straightway into the social New Jerusalem

かれらは、プロレタリアートが社会的新エルサレムにまっす
ぐに行進することを強く望んでいる

but in reality it requires the proletariat to remain within the
bounds of existing society

しかし、現実には、プロレタリアートが既存の社会の枠内に
とどまることを要求する

they ask the proletariat to cast away all their hateful ideas
concerning the Bourgeoisie

かれらは、プロレタリアートに、ブルジョアジーに関するす
べての憎悪に満ちた考えを捨て去るよう求めている

there is a second more practical, but less systematic, form of
this Socialism

この社会主義には、より実際的ではあるが、あまり体系的で
はない第二の形態がある

this form of socialism sought to depreciate every
revolutionary movement in the eyes of the working class

この形態の社会主義は、労働者階級の目から見て、あらゆる
革命運動を貶めようとした

they argue no mere political reform could be of any

advantage to them
彼らは、単なる政治改革は彼らにとって何の利益にもならないと主張する

only a change in the material conditions of existence in economic relations are of benefit
経済関係における物質的存在条件の変化だけが有益である

like communism, this form of socialism advocates for a change in the material conditions of existence
共産主義のように、この形態の社会主義は、存在の物質的条件の変化を提唱しています

however, this form of socialism by no means suggests the abolition of the Bourgeoisie relations of production
しかし、この社会主義の形態は、決してブルジョアジー的生産関係の廃止を示唆するものではない

the abolition of the Bourgeoisie relations of production can only be achieved through a revolution
ブルジョアジー的生産関係の廃止は、革命によってのみ達成されうる

but instead of a revolution, this form of socialism suggests administrative reforms
しかし、この形態の社会主義は、革命ではなく、行政改革を示唆している

and these administrative reforms would be based on the continued existence of these relations
そして、これらの行政改革は、これらの関係の存続を基礎としている

reforms, therefore, that in no respect affect the relations between capital and labour
したがって、資本と労働の関係にいかなる点においても影響を与えない改革

at best, such reforms lessen the cost and simplify the administrative work of Bourgeoisie government
せいぜい、そのような改革は、ブルジョアジー政府の費用を軽減し、行政業務を単純化するにすぎない

Bourgeois Socialism attains adequate expression, when, and only when, it becomes a mere figure of speech
ブルジョア社会主義は、それが単なる言論の形象になったと

きにのみ、適切な表現を獲得する

Free trade: for the benefit of the working class

自由貿易:労働者階級の利益のために

Protective duties: for the benefit of the working class

保護義務:労働者階級の利益のために

Prison Reform: for the benefit of the working class

刑務所改革:労働者階級の利益のために

This is the last word and the only seriously meant word of Bourgeoisie Socialism

これはブルジョアジー社会主義の最後の言葉であり、唯一の真剣に意味された言葉である

It is summed up in the phrase: the Bourgeoisie is a Bourgeoisie for the benefit of the working class

それは、「ブルジョアジーは労働者階級の利益のためのブルジョアジーである」という言葉に要約されている

Critical-Utopian Socialism and Communism
批判的ユートピア社会主義と共産主義

We do not here refer to that literature which has always given voice to the demands of the proletariat

われわれはここで、つねにプロレタリアートの要求に声をあげてきた文学に言及しているのではない

this has been present in every great modern revolution, such as the writings of Babeuf and others

これは、バブーフや他の人々の著作など、すべての偉大な近代革命に存在してきました

The first direct attempts of the proletariat to attain its own ends necessarily failed

プロレタリアートが自らの目的を達成しようとする最初の直接の試みは、必然的に失敗した

these attempts were made in times of universal excitement, when feudal society was being overthrown

これらの試みは、封建社会が打倒されつつあった普遍的な興奮の時代に行われました

the then undeveloped state of the proletariat led to those attempts failing

当時のプロレタリアートの未発達な状態は、これらの試みの失敗につながった

and they failed due to the absence of the economic conditions for its emancipation

そして、彼らは、その解放のための経済的条件がなかったため、失敗した

conditions that had yet to be produced, and could be produced by the impending Bourgeoisie epoch alone

まだ生み出されていなかった諸条件、そして差し迫ったブルジョアジー時代によってのみ生み出されうる諸条件

The revolutionary literature that accompanied these first movements of the proletariat had necessarily a reactionary character

プロレタリアートのこれらの最初の運動に付随した革命的文学は、必然的に反動的な性格を持っていた

This literature inculcated universal asceticism and social

levelling in its crudest form
この文学は、普遍的な禁欲主義と社会的平準化を最も粗雑な
形で教え込んだ

**The Socialist and Communist systems, properly so called,
spring into existence in the early undeveloped period**
社会主義と共産主義の制度は、正しくはそう呼ばれているが
、未発達の初期に出現した

**Saint-Simon, Fourier, Owen and others, described the
struggle between proletariat and Bourgeoisie (see Section 1)**
サン・シモン、フーリエ、オーウェンらは、プロレタリアー
トとブルジョアジーの闘争を描いた(第1節参照)

**The founders of these systems see, indeed, the class
antagonisms**
これらの制度の創始者たちは、実に階級対立を見ている

**they also see the action of the decomposing elements, in the
prevailing form of society**
彼らはまた、社会の支配的な形態において、分解する要素の
作用を見ます

**But the proletariat, as yet in its infancy, offers to them the
spectacle of a class without any historical initiative**
しかし、プロレタリアートは、まだその初期段階にあり、彼
らに、いかなる歴史的主導権も持たない階級の見世物を提供
している

**they see the spectacle of a social class without any
independent political movement**
彼らは、独立した政治運動のない社会階級の光景を見ている

**the development of class antagonism keeps even pace with
the development of industry**
階級対立の発展は、産業の発展と歩調を合わせている

**so the economic situation does not as yet offer to them the
material conditions for the emancipation of the proletariat**
したがって、経済状況は、プロレタリアートの解放のための
物質的条件をまだ彼らに提供していない

**They therefore search after a new social science, after new
social laws, that are to create these conditions**
それゆえ、彼らは、これらの条件をつくりだす新しい社会科
学、新しい社会法則を追い求める

historical action is to yield to their personal inventive action
歴史的行為は、彼らの個人的な創意工夫の行動に屈服することである

historically created conditions of emancipation are to yield to fantastic conditions
歴史的に作り出された解放の条件は、幻想的な条件に屈服することである

and the gradual, spontaneous class-organisation of the proletariat is to yield to the organisation of society
そして、プロレタリアートの漸進的で自発的な階級組織は、社会の組織に屈服することである

the organisation of society specially contrived by these inventors
これらの発明者によって特別に考案された社会の組織

Future history resolves itself, in their eyes, into the propaganda and the practical carrying out of their social plans
未来の歴史は、彼らの目には、プロパガンダと彼らの社会計画の実際的な実行に解決される

In the formation of their plans they are conscious of caring chiefly for the interests of the working class
かれらは、かれらの計画の形成において、主として労働者階級の利益を気遣うことを意識している

Only from the point of view of being the most suffering class does the proletariat exist for them
プロレタリアートは、最も苦しむ階級であるという観点からのみ、彼らのために存在するのである

The undeveloped state of the class struggle and their own surroundings inform their opinions
階級闘争の未発達な状態と彼ら自身の環境は、彼らの意見を知らせます

Socialists of this kind consider themselves far superior to all class antagonisms
この種の社会主義者は、自分たちがあらゆる階級対立よりはるかに優れていると考えている

They want to improve the condition of every member of society, even that of the most favoured

彼らは、社会のあらゆる構成員の状態を改善したいと願っています

Hence, they habitually appeal to society at large, without distinction of class

それゆえ、彼らは階級の区別なく、社会全体にアピールする習慣があるのです

nay, they appeal to society at large by preference to the ruling class

いや、彼らは支配階級を優先することで、社会全体にアピールしている

to them, all it requires is for others to understand their system

彼らにとって必要なのは、他の人が彼らのシステムを理解することだけです

because how can people fail to see that the best possible plan is for the best possible state of society?

なぜなら、可能な限り最善の計画が、社会の可能な限り最良の状態のためのものであることを、どうして人々が見落とすことができるのでしょうか?

Hence, they reject all political, and especially all revolutionary, action

それゆえ、彼らはすべての政治的行動、特にすべての革命的行動を拒絶する

they wish to attain their ends by peaceful means

彼らは平和的な手段によって目的を達成することを望んでいます

they endeavour, by small experiments, which are necessarily doomed to failure

彼らは、必然的に失敗する運命にある小さな実験によって努力します

and by the force of example they try to pave the way for the new social Gospel

そして、模範の力によって、新しい社会的な福音への道を開こうとします

Such fantastic pictures of future society, painted at a time when the proletariat is still in a very undeveloped state

プロレタリアートがまだ非常に未発達な状態にある時代に描

かれた、未来社会の幻想的な絵

and it still has but a fantastical conception of its own position
そして、それはまだ、それ自身の立場についての空想的な概念しか持っていません

but their first instinctive yearnings correspond with the yearnings of the proletariat
しかし、彼らの最初の本能的な憧れは、プロレタリアートの憧れと一致している

both yearn for a general reconstruction of society
両者とも社会の全般的な再建を切望している

But these Socialist and Communist publications also contain a critical element
しかし、これらの社会主義と共産主義の出版物には、重要な要素も含まれています

They attack every principle of existing society
彼らは既存の社会のあらゆる原則を攻撃します

Hence they are full of the most valuable materials for the enlightenment of the working class
それゆえ、それらは労働者階級の啓蒙のための最も貴重な資料に満ちている

they propose abolition of the distinction between town and country, and the family
彼らは、町と田舎、家族の区別の廃止を提案しています

the abolition of the carrying on of industries for the account of private individuals
私人による産業の営養の廃止

and the abolition of the wage system and the proclamation of social harmony
賃金制度の廃止と社会的調和の宣言

the conversion of the functions of the State into a mere superintendence of production
国家の機能を単なる生産監督者に転用すること

all these proposals, point solely to the disappearance of class antagonisms
これらすべての提案は、階級対立の消滅のみを指し示している

class antagonisms were, at that time, only just cropping up
当時、階級対立は始まったばかりでした

in these publications these class antagonisms are recognised in their earliest, indistinct and undefined forms only
これらの出版物では、これらの階級対立は、最も初期の、不明瞭で、未定義の形でのみ認識されている

These proposals, therefore, are of a purely Utopian character
したがって、これらの提案は純粋にユートピア的な性格のものです

The significance of Critical-Utopian Socialism and Communism bears an inverse relation to historical development
批判的ユートピア的社会主義と共産主義の意義は、歴史的発展と反比例する

the modern class struggle will develop and continue to take definite shape
現代の階級闘争は発展し、一定の形をとり続けるであろう

this fantastic standing from the contest will lose all practical value
コンテストでのこの素晴らしい地位は、すべての実用的な価値を失います

these fantastic attacks on class antagonisms will lose all theoretical justification
階級対立に対するこれらの幻想的な攻撃は、あらゆる理論的正当性を失うだろう

the originators of these systems were, in many respects, revolutionary
これらのシステムの創始者は、多くの点で革命的でした

but their disciples have, in every case, formed mere reactionary sects
しかし、彼らの弟子たちは、いずれの場合も、単なる反動的な宗派を形成してきた

They hold tightly to the original views of their masters
彼らは主人の元の見解をしっかりと保持しています

but these views are in opposition to the progressive historical development of the proletariat
しかし、これらの見解は、プロレタリアートの進歩的な歴史

的発展に反対するものである

They, therefore, endeavour, and that consistently, to deaden the class struggle

それゆえ、彼らは階級闘争を鎮めようと努力し、それを一貫して行っている

and they consistently endeavour to reconcile the class antagonisms

そして、かれらは、一貫して階級対立を和解させようと努力する

They still dream of experimental realisation of their social Utopias

彼らはいまだに、自分たちの社会的なユートピアの実験的な実現を夢見ている

they still dream of founding isolated "phalansteres" and establishing "Home Colonies"

彼らはいまだに孤立した「ファランステル」を創設し、「ホームコロニー」を設立することを夢見ている

they dream of setting up a "Little Icaria"—duodecimo editions of the New Jerusalem

彼らは「リトル・イカリア」、つまり新しいエルサレムの十二階版を建てることを夢見ています

and they dream to realise all these castles in the air

そして、彼らは空中にあるこれらすべての城を実現することを夢見ています

they are compelled to appeal to the feelings and purses of the bourgeois

彼らはブルジョアジーの感情と財布に訴えることを余儀なくされている

By degrees they sink into the category of the reactionary conservative Socialists depicted above

程度によって、彼らは上に描かれた反動的な保守社会主義者の範疇に沈む

they differ from these only by more systematic pedantry

それらは、より体系的な衒学によってのみこれらと異なります

and they differ by their fanatical and superstitious belief in the miraculous effects of their social science

そして、彼らは、社会科学の奇跡的な効果に対する狂信的で迷信的な信念によって異なる

They, therefore, violently oppose all political action on the part of the working class

それゆえ、彼らは労働者階級の側のあらゆる政治的行動に激しく反対する

such action, according to them, can only result from blind unbelief in the new Gospel

彼らによれば、そのような行動は、新しい福音に対する盲目的な不信仰からしか生じ得ません

The Owenites in England, and the Fourierists in France, respectively, oppose the Chartists and the "Réformistes"

イギリスのオーウェン派とフランスのフーリエ主義者は、それぞれチャーティストと「レフォルミスト」に反対している

Position of the Communists in Relation to the Various Existing Opposition Parties
既存の様々な反対政党に対する共産主義者の立場

Section II has made clear the relations of the Communists to the existing working-class parties
第2節は、共産主義者と既存の労働者階級の諸政党との関係を明らかにした

such as the Chartists in England, and the Agrarian Reformers in America
イギリスのチャーティストやアメリカの農地改革者など

The Communists fight for the attainment of the immediate aims
共産党員は当面の目標達成のために闘う

they fight for the enforcement of the momentary interests of the working class
彼らは労働者階級の一時的な利益の執行のために闘う

but in the political movement of the present, they also represent and take care of the future of that movement
しかし、現在の政治運動において、彼らはまた、その運動の将来を代表し、世話をします

In France the Communists ally themselves with the Social-Democrats
フランスでは、共産主義者は社会民主党と同盟を結んでいる

and they position themselves against the conservative and radical Bourgeoisie
そして、彼らは保守的で急進的なブルジョアジーに対抗する立場をとっています

however, they reserve the right to take up a critical position in regard to phrases and illusions traditionally handed down from the great Revolution
しかし、彼らは、大革命から伝統的に受け継がれてきた言葉や幻想に関して、批判的な立場をとる権利を留保する

In Switzerland they support the Radicals, without losing sight of the fact that this party consists of antagonistic elements
スイスでは、彼らは急進派を支持しているが、この党が敵対

的な要素で構成されているという事実を見失うことはない

partly of Democratic Socialists, in the French sense, partly of radical Bourgeoisie

一部は民主社会主義者、フランス的な意味では、一部は急進的ブルジョアジー

In Poland they support the party that insists on an agrarian revolution as the prime condition for national emancipation

ポーランドでは、民族解放の第一条件として農業革命を主張する政党を支持している

that party which fomented the insurrection of Cracow in 1846

1846年にクラクフの反乱を扇動した党

In Germany they fight with the Bourgeoisie whenever it acts in a revolutionary way

ドイツでは、ブルジョアジーが革命的なやり方で行動するたびに、ブルジョアジーと闘う

against the absolute monarchy, the feudal squirearchy, and the petty Bourgeoisie

絶対君主制、封建的従者制、小ブルジョアジーに対して

But they never cease, for a single instant, to instil into the working class one particular idea

しかし、彼らは一瞬たりとも、労働者階級に特定の考えを植え付けることをやめない

the clearest possible recognition of the hostile antagonism between Bourgeoisie and proletariat

ブルジョアジーとプロレタリアートの敵対関係を可能な限り明確に認識すること

so that the German workers may straightaway use the weapons at their disposal

そうすれば、ドイツ人労働者は、すぐに武器を使えるようになる

the social and political conditions that the Bourgeoisie must necessarily introduce along with its supremacy

ブルジョアジーがその優越性とともに必然的に導入しなければならない社会的および政治的条件

the fall of the reactionary classes in Germany is inevitable

ドイツにおける反動階級の没落は不可避である

and then the fight against the Bourgeoisie itself may immediately begin

そうすれば、ブルジョアジーそのものに対する闘いが直ちに始まるかもしれない

The Communists turn their attention chiefly to Germany, because that country is on the eve of a Bourgeoisie revolution

共産主義者が主としてドイツに注意を向けるのは、ドイツがブルジョアジー革命の前夜にあるからである

a revolution that is bound to be carried out under more advanced conditions of European civilisation

ヨーロッパ文明のより進んだ条件の下で遂行されるに違いない革命

and it is bound to be carried out with a much more developed proletariat

そして、それははるかに発達したプロレタリアートによって遂行されるに違いない

a proletariat more advanced than that of England was in the seventeenth, and of France in the eighteenth century

17世紀にはイギリス、18世紀にはフランスよりも進んだプロレタリアートがいた

and because the Bourgeoisie revolution in Germany will be but the prelude to an immediately following proletarian revolution

なぜなら、ドイツにおけるブルジョアジー革命は、その直後のプロレタリア革命の序曲にすぎないからである

In short, the Communists everywhere support every revolutionary movement against the existing social and political order of things

要するに、共産主義者は、あらゆる場所で、既存の社会的、政治的秩序に反対するあらゆる革命運動を支持しているのである

In all these movements they bring to the front, as the leading question in each, the property question

これらすべての動きにおいて、彼らは、それぞれの主要な問題として、財産の問題を前面に押し出します

no matter what its degree of development is in that country

at the time
当時のその国の発展の度合いがどうであれ

Finally, they labour everywhere for the union and agreement of the democratic parties of all countries
最後に、彼らはすべての国の民主政党の団結と合意のためにあらゆる場所で働いています

The Communists disdain to conceal their views and aims
共産主義者は、自分たちの見解や目的を隠すことを軽蔑する

They openly declare that their ends can be attained only by the forcible overthrow of all existing social conditions
彼らは、現存するすべての社会状況を強制的に打倒することによってのみ、その目的を達成できると公然と宣言している

Let the ruling classes tremble at a Communistic revolution
支配階級を共産主義革命に震え上がらせよう

The proletarians have nothing to lose but their chains
プロレタリア階級は、その鎖以外に失うものは何もない

They have a world to win
彼らには勝つべき世界がある

WORKING MEN OF ALL COUNTRIES, UNITE!
すべての国の働く男性、団結せよ!